Faith and Works

Cranmer and Hooker on Justification

Philip Edgcumbe Hughes

Morehouse-Barlow Co., Inc.
Wilton, Connecticut 06897

Morehouse-Barlow Co., Inc.
78 Danbury Road
Wilton, Connecticut 06897

ISBN 0-8192-1315-2
Library of Congress Catalog Card Number 82-61273
Printed in the United States of America

For

CHRISTOPHER FITZSIMONS ALLISON

Bishop of South Carolina

and

CHARLES BRINKLEY MORTON

Bishop of San Diego

'Our justification doth come freely by the mere mercy of God, and of so great and free mercy that, whereas all the world was not able of themselves to pay any part towards their ransom, it pleased our heavenly Father of his infinite mercy, without any our desert or deserving, to prepare for us the most precious jewels of Christ's body and blood, whereby our ransom might be fully paid, the law fulfilled, and his justice fully satisfied. So that Christ is now the righteousness of all that truly do believe in him.'

THOMAS CRANMER

'The righteousness wherewith we shall be clothed in the world to come is both perfect and inherent. That whereby we are justified is perfect, but not inherent. That whereby we are sanctified, inherent, but not perfect.'

'The best things we do have somewhat in them to be pardoned. How then can we do anything meritorious and worthy to be rewarded?'

'Faith is the only hand which putteth on Christ unto justification, and Christ the only garment which, being so put on, covereth the shame of our defiled natures.'

RICHARD HOOKER

Contents

I

Introduction

A central issue in the controversy between the reforming leaders of the Church of England and the theologians of the Church of Rome in the sixteenth century concerned the manner of the sinner's justification before God. Was it possible and necessary for a person to contribute to and thereby in some measure to be deserving of his own justification by the cultivation of virtues and the performance of good works? Are good works in themselves meritorious in such a way that divine grace is owed to them? Or is the justification of the sinner due entirely to the unmerited grace of God which is appropriated solely by faith in the perfection of Christ's work of redemption? What was at stake in the debate over these questions was the right understanding of the Gospel. Consequently, the right answer to them has continued to be a matter of perennial importance for the Christian Church. The response of classical Anglicanism has been clearly given by Thomas Cranmer and Richard Hooker, the two outstanding architects of the doctrine of the Church of England in the Henrician/Edwardian and Elizabethan periods respectively. They will speak for themselves in the writings from their pens on the theme of justification which are included in this volume.

Neither Cranmer nor Hooker claimed in any sense to be the originators or first formulators of the teaching they propounded. Quite the contrary; for, though they were charged with the invention of novel notions, it was their confident and constant claim (and the claim also of their colleagues) that their teaching was precisely that of the New Testament and that they had the support of the church fathers — as the discussion that follows will show. Their intention, moreover, was not merely to advocate the doctrine of the Church of

England but also to restore to the Christian Church at large important truths which had long been covered over or compromised.

It must be said, further, that the reforming movement in the Church of England developed from its own indigenous roots. In its origins it was not something imported from elsewhere. This is a matter of historical fact rather than ultimate significance, for it is the truth itself that is important far beyond its geographical derivation. It is, however, a fact of some interest which serves to discredit the charge once made that the shaping of Anglicanism in the sixteenth century was something alien and un-English. Certainly, in the course of its formulation Anglicanism was receptive of influences that crossed the English Channel, just as its own distinctive force was felt and appreciated beyond the limits of its own native territory. But this mutual susceptibility was the result of discovering that in the spontaneous surge of renewal, both in England and beyond, there was an essential harmony of belief, not least respecting the doctrine of justification, and that this congenial spirit sprang from the recovery of the evangelical truth of the New Testament.

Wycliffe and the Lollards

The universal acknowledgment by the early Church of the canonical authority of Holy Scripture defined not only the standard to which the Church ought always to conform but also the principle in accordance with which the Church ought always to be ready to reform itself. Significantly, the Church's inner history has in general been blighted by a propensity on the part of ecclesiastical authoritarianism to usurp the throne of biblical authority, and the recurring task of reform has consisted in the need to reaffirm the latter. In medieval England this principle of renewal was boldly asserted by John Wycliffe (d. 1384). On the subject of authority, as Gotthard Lechler has observed, "Wycliffe approves himself as a thoroughly independent thinker, and especially as a man imbued with the spirit of the Reformation; for he has already come in sight of the principle that Holy Scripture is the only authoritative document of revelation, that is the rule and standard of all teachings and teachers."[1] For Wycliffe, the authority of Scripture flowed from the premise that the word of Scripture is the Word of God, and as such the seed of regeneration and the bread of life which, while indispensable indeed to the theologian, is no less necessary for the layman and the humblest of citizens. Hence the high priority he assigned to the translation of the Bible into the language of the people.[2]

With regard to the question of the sinner's justification before God, Wycliffe firmly denied that this could in any way be merited by the good works of the creature: citing the admonition of Christ, "When you have done all that is commanded you, say, 'We are unworthy servants: we have only done what it was our duty to do'" (Luke 17:10), he explained that even the most meticulous fulfillment of all God's commands contributed nothing to God and that in any case all one's abilities were given by "the mere grace of God" and all one's achievements owed to his prevenient and continuing help.[3] Again, adducing the question posed by St. Paul, "What do you have that you have not received?" (1 Cor.4:7), he insisted that "it is impossible for a creature to serve God even in the slightest degree apart from the bestowal of grace, with the consequence that a creature can merit absolutely nothing from God *ex condigno*."[4] Nor can creaturely merit cancel sin: "I reckon," Wycliffe wrote, "that it is impossible for even the smallest sin committed against the Lord to be removed by any merit unless it is removed sovereignly by the merit of this Man."[5] Accordingly, he denied both the possibility that sinful man could contribute meritoriously to his justification or regeneration and also the possibility of there being a heavenly 'bank" of surplus or supererogatory merit, an accumulation of the excessive worthiness of the great saints, which could be drawn upon by those whose sanctity was deficient — a notion he denounced as the "lying fiction of a limitless treasury of the supererogatory merit of the church triumphant which the pope is empowered to distribute."[6]

The influence of Wycliffe's thought and example continued to be strong in the hearts of his followers the Lollards, who were eager students of the English translation of the Bible initiated by their master, and who maintained a solid, though mostly quiet, presence in many different parts of the land. From time to time there were prosecutions of those of their number who ventured to be outspokenly critical of what they regarded as ecclesiastical abuses.[7] The Lollards form an indigenous and not unimportant line that stretches over a century and a half from Wycliffe to Cranmer. As A.G. Dickens has stated, "the ingredients of early Protestantism proved already numerous in the reign of Henry VIII," and "we may nowadays confidently ascribe a role of some importance on the popular level to the still vital force of Lollardy."[8] Similarly, William Clebsch has declared that "from the outset English Protestantism was shaped by the waning Wycliffites whom it engulfed."[9]

That Wycliffe was held in veneration and his teachings cherished for generations after his death by numbers of persons, some learned and exalted, many of humble estate, is amply attested in the annals of the fifteenth century. By way of example, we give here the testimony of William Thorpe, who, when arraigned before the Archbishop of Canterbury, Thomas Arundel, in 1407, spoke as follows:

> Sir, Master John Wycliffe was holden of full many men the greatest clerk that they knew then living; and therewith he was named a passing ruly man and an innocent in his living: and therefore great men communed oft with him, and they loved so his learning that they wrote it and busily enforced them to rule themselves thereafter. Therefore, Sir, this foresaid learning of M. John Wycliffe is yet holden of full many men and women the most agreeable learning unto the living and teaching of Christ and of his apostles, and most openly showing and declaring how the Church of Christ hath been, and yet should be, ruled and governed. Therefore so many men and women covet this learning, and purpose, through God's grace, to conform their living like to this learning of Wycliffe. . . . And so, before all other men, I chose willingly to be informed of them and by them, and specially of Wycliffe himself, as of the most virtuous and godly wise man that I heard of or knew.[10]

John Colet

Before the dawn of the sixteenth century another powerful voice was raised in England. This was the voice of John Colet, who in 1497 began the series of public lectures on

Paul's Epistle to the Romans and First Epistle to the Corinthians which attracted a large and enthusiastic audience. These expositions, which shunned the elaborate allegorism that had for long fascinated the scholastic mind and explained the scriptural text in a natural and straightforward manner, have justly been described as "a milestone in the history of Christian scholarship,"[11] and as "marking an era in the history of religious thought in England."[12] In his subsequent career as dean of St. Paul's Cathedral Colet's reputation as an outspoken and challenging preacher continued undiminished. Of particular interest to us in this study is the clear manner in which he propounded the doctrine of justification by faith. It was with the firmest emphasis that he taught that the sinner is justified not at all by any supposed human merit but solely by the freely given grace of God through faith in Jesus Christ. God, he affirmed, "of his grace imparts himself to those who believe and trust in him, who have also been taken and drawn away by him from unbelief, that they may trust in him alone, and believe that by no other means whatever can they be justified than by the divine grace."[13]

The history of Abraham, as St. Paul shows, illustrates the truth that justification is by faith, not by works: "Abraham," Colet declares, "had testimony borne to his righteousness before the works and ceremonies of the Law were ordained, that it might be clearly taught that justification belongs not to those who do works under the Law, but to those who imitate the faith of Abraham."Accordingly, the Apostle "concludes that, being justified by faith, and trusting in God alone, men are reconciled to God through Jesus Christ, and restored to grace, that they may stand before God, and themselves remain sons of God, and look for the certain glory of the sons of God . . . . For it is of the great love and grace of God toward us that we have been reconciled. Otherwise his Son would not have died for us, even when we were ungodly and at enmity with God."[14] Indeed, "it is God's will that his loving-kindness and mercy and benefits should be acknowledged to proceed wholly and manifestly from himself; that men may have no room for either pride or idle questioning, but may own that nothing is of themselves, everything from God."[15] To the same effect is the apostolic teaching that "all things are done for men by the promise and free election of God, they themselves contributing nothing towards that election, lest the counsel and purpose of God should seem to depend on the will and deeds of men." It follows, then, that, "whatever there is which affects the blessedness of mankind, it rests wholly upon the purpose and will and grace of God,"[16] and that "none can now truly say that he is saved except by grace."[17]

It is not good works that earn grace, but grace that begets good works. Justification comes first, then sanctification. "We are not righteous through observance of the law," says Colet "but we observe the good law because we are righteous."[18] Otherwise expressed, "the love of God within us is kindled from God's love toward us, and is begotten in us by a loving God; . . . hence it is by God's loving us that we love him in return."[19] If it is true that "there is nothing in man but the justest cause of death, nothing to deserve grace, but only to provoke wrath,"[20] then it follows that "the man who would be safe and sound must rest in the grace and love of God alone."[21] There is no dismissal of good works, except as a cause of the sinner's justification. The good works of righteous living, however, should follow justification as a natural consequence. Our justification, Colet asserts, is "to the end that we should live righteously." Accordingly:

> Our justification precedes the righteous dealing which is an observance of the law, and we do not act righteously before we ourselves are righteous. Of our own human and carnal nature we are all unrighteous, confessedly powerless to do anything aright, though righteous deeds are enjoined upon us. What indeed is the use of enjoining precepts on the unrighteous, unless we first make them righteous, so that, being made righteous, they may be able to observe the precepts of righteousness?[22]

There is no question that the doctrine proclaimed by Colet was influential. His preaching both at Oxford and subsequently in London drew large and eager crowds from all walks of life, and it is hard to believe that his emphasis on justification through divine grace alone was not a seed which found lodgment in the minds of some who after his death would energetically expound this doctrine and insist on its importance for the spiritual renewal of the Church. It is, for example, reasonable to suppose that William Tyndale when he was an undergraduate at Magdalen Hall must have been among the hearers of Colet's Oxford lectures.[23] The influence of Colet may perhaps be discerned behind the information given by Foxe that Tyndale was "brought up from a child in the University of Oxford, where he, by long continuance, grew up and increased as well in the knowledge of tongues, and other liberal arts, as especially in the knowledge of the Scriptures."[24] There are passages in the sermons of Hugh Latimer where an indebtedness to the preaching of Colet has been postulated.[25] It has also been rightly pointed out concerning the articles alleged against Robert Barnes as heretical in 1526 that "no point in the articles derived from Luther more than from Wycliffe or Hus or Colet."[26] According to Erasmus, his close friend, Colet had read the writings of Wyclife,[27] and it is not entirely surprising that Colet was suspected and accused, unsuccessfully, by hostile spirits of propounding views sympathetic to Lollardism. We know that those of Lollard persuasion approved of his preaching and encouraged people to listen to his sermons.[28] Latimer, in fact, when preaching in 1552, recalled the time "when Doctor Colet was in trouble, and should have been burnt, if God had not turned the king's heart to the contrary."[29]

Thomas Bilney

Of some interest is the fact not only that it was Colet who induced Erasmus to undertake the preparation of a new Latin translation of the New Testament but also that in 1519, the year of Colet's death, Thomas Bilney in Cambridge, attracted by the fame of Erasmus as a master of elegant Latin prose, experienced an evangelical conversion when reading a copy of the second edition of this *Novum Instrumentum* (published with the revised Greek text and Erasmus's Latin version in parallel columns). Bilney, himself already a scholarly priest of the Church, described the occasion in a letter to the Bishop of London, Cuthbert Tonstal, in the following manner:

At last I heard speak of Jesus, even then when the New Testament was first set forth by Erasmus; which when

I understood to be eloquently done by him, being allured rather by the Latin than by the word of God (for at that I time I knew not what it meant), I bought it even by the providence of God, as I do now well understand and perceive: and at the first reading (as I well remember) I chanced upon this sentence of St. Paul (O most sweet and comfortable sentence to my soul!) in 1 Tim.i, 'It is a true saying, and worthy of all men to be embraced, that Christ Jesus came into the world to save sinners, of whom I am the chief and principal.' This one sentence, through God's instruction and inward working, which I did not then perceive, did so exhilarate my heart, being before wounded with the guilt of my sins, and being almost in despair, that immediately I felt a marvellous comfort and quietness, insomuch 'that my bruised bones leaped for joy.'[30]

"After this," Bilney continues,

the Scripture began to be more pleasant unto me than the honey or the honeycomb; wherein I learned that all my travails, all my fasting and watching, all the redemption of masses and pardons, being done without trust in Christ, who only saveth his people from their sins; these, I say, I learned to be nothing else but even (as St. Augustine saith) a hasty and swift running out of the right way; . . . neither could I be relieved or eased of the sharp stings and bitings of my sins before I was taught of God that lesson which Christ speaketh of in John iii: 'Even as Moses exalted the serpent in the desert, so shall the Son of Man be exalted, that all who believe in him should not perish, but have life everlasting.'

Bilney went on to affirm, "with all my whole power," as absolutely necessary, "that all men should first acknowledge their sins, and condemn them, and afterwards hunger and thirst for that righteousness whereof St. Paul speaketh: 'The righteousness of God, by faith in Jesus Christ, is upon all them who believe in him; for there is no difference: for all have sinned and lack the glory of God, and are justified freely through his grace, by the redemption which is in Christ Jesus.'[31]

It was thus that Bilney came with some suddenness to an understanding of the apostolic doctrine of justification.

Foxe writes of Bilney that, "as he himself was greatly inflamed with the love of true religion and godliness, even so again was in his heart an incredible desire to allure many unto the same, desiring nothing more than that he might stir up and encourage any to the love of Christ and sincere religion." Nor, Foxe observes, "were his labours vain; for he converted many of his fellows unto the knowledge of the Gospel."[32] He was a leading spirit in the coterie of scholars who used to meet for Christian fellowship and Bible study at the White Horse Inn in Cambridge, and has been described as "the first framer of that university in the knowledge of Christ."[33] Among those whom he was instrumental in bringing to conversion were Hugh Latimer, John Lambert and Robert Barnes. All three, like Bilney, were scholars and priests, and all three, like Bilney, sooner or later suffered death by burning.[34]

George Joye

A fellow of Peterhouse, George Joye was another member of this Cambridge circle. He went on to play an important role as a biblical translator and as the author and publisher of numerous theological treatises. Of particular interest for our present purpose in his *Answer to Ashwell*, which appeared in 1531, the year of Bilney's martyrdom, and clearly expounds the doctrine of justification by faith apart from works.[35] Joye denied that justification was dependent on the infusion of divine grace and the performance of good works, affirming, on the contrary, that it flows from the mercy and faithfulness of God as manifested in Christ's atoning self-sacrifice in the sinner's place.

> The righteousness which is allowed before God that cometh of faith is sometimes in Scripture called his mercy or favour towards us and in us, whereby he is moved for Christ's blood's sake to promise us forgiveness, and sometimes it is taken for his truth and faithfulness in the performing of his promise, and of this he is called just, righteous, faithful, and true.[36]

Though Joye disallowed good works as being in themselves meritorious and laying a claim upon divine reward,

he insisted on their importance as the fruit and evidence of
a true faith.

> Faith is an infallible and undoubted certainty in our
> hearts, whereby we believe and trust in the invisible
> God. . . . Faith is that same constant and fast persua-
> sion in our hearts assured us by the Holy Ghost, certify-
> ing us of the goodness of God and of his promises
> toward us, by the which persuasion we believe verily
> his words and are assured in our hearts (the Holy Ghost
> testifying it in us) that he is our God, our Father, to us
> an almighty helper and deliverer, and that we are
> received into his favour by the death and merits of his
> Son Jesus Christ our Saviour, upon the which belief
> and assured persuasion we love him so earnestly again
> that we cease not (the occasion and time offered) to
> fulfil his pleasures in doing the works of love or charity
> to our neighbours.[37]

Robert Barnes

At the time of his conversion Robert Barnes was prior of
the Augustinian friary at Cambridge. In 1528 he sought
refuge on the Continent from his persecutors in England,
and on his return to his homeland some three years later he
brought with him not only an appeal to the English king
with the title *A supplication made by Robert Barnes, doctor
in divinity, unto the most excellent and redoubted prince
King Henry VIII* but also a treatise on justification by faith
which he had composed and had printed when in exile. The
latter is an important exposition of the reformed doctrine of
the manner of the sinner's justification before God. Barnes
stresses that our righteousness before God is entirely in
Christ and not at all in ourselves, and therefore that all our
trust must be in Christ and not even in the smallest degree
in ourselves.

> If we will truly confess Christ, then must we grant with
> our hearts that Christ is all our justice, all our redemp-
> tion, all our wisdom, all our holiness, all alone the pur-
> chaser of grace, alone the peacemaker between God
> and man; briefly, all goodness that we have, that it is of
> him, by him, and for his sake only; and that we have

need of nothing towards our salvation, but of him only, and we desire no other salvation, nor any other satisfaction, nor any help of any other creature, either heavenly or earthly, but of him only; for, as St. Peter saith, there is no other name given unto men wherein they must be saved. And also St. Paul saith, by him are all that believe justified from all things. Moreover St. John witnesseth the same, in these words: He it is that hath obtained grace for our sins; and in another place: He sent his Son to make agreement for our sins.[38]

Referring to the apocalyptic vision in which the Lamb alone was found worthy to open the book in heaven and was worshipped with the praise of the "new song": "Thou art worthy, for thou wast killed and hast redeemed us with thy blood,"[39] Barnes asks: "Now what cause lay you for your good works?," and answers:

The Lamb hath alone died for us, the Lamb only hath shed his blood for us; these things hath he done alone. Now if these be sufficient, then hath he alone made satisfaction and is alone worthy to be our redeemer and justifier.

Citing Romans 3:23f. (as we have seen Bilney did before him) where St. Paul declares: "All men are sinners and want the glory of God, but they are justified freely by his grace through the redemption that is in Christ Jesus," he pursues his argument as follows:

What is this, that all men have sinned, yea, and are justified freely? How shall a sinner do good works? How can he deserve to be justified? What call you, freely? If there be any deservings less or more, then it is not freely. What call you, by his grace? If it be any part of works, then it is not of grace. For, as St. Paul saith, then grace were not grace.[40] Here can be no evasion, the words are so plain. If you bring in any help of works, then for so much our redemption is not freely, nor yet is it of grace, as concerneth the part that cometh of works, but partly of works, and then do you destroy all St. Paul and his whole disputation. For he contends against works, and clearly excludes works in justification, and brings in grace only.

Barnes adduces strong patristic support from the writings of Ambrose, Augustine, Tertullian, Origen and Bernard, though his first and final authority is the teaching of Christ and his apostles, as he insists that "no manner of works, whether they are in faith or out of faith, can help to justify." "Wherefore," he asserts,

> I conclude of these scriptures and of these doctors that the faith which we have in Christ Jesus, and his blessed blood, doth only, and sufficiently, justify us before God, without the help of any works.

He is no less emphatic, however, that this is not a prescription for antinomianism or selfish and unworthy living. The very faith that justifies is freely and graciously given by God,[41] and it is inconceivable that it should be conducive to ungodly inactivity.

> Because it is given from heaven into our hearts by the Spirit of God, therefore it can be no idle thing; but it must needs do all manner of things that are to the honour of God and also to the profit of our neighbour. . . . But these works are not done to justify the man, but a just man must needs do them . . . . And as a good tree in time of the year brings forth good apples, not to make it good, for it is good before, nor yet is this apple to its profit, but unto others, notwithstanding, the good nature that is in it must needs bring it forth — so likewise the just man must needs do good works, not by them to be justified, but only in them to serve his brother: for he hath no need of them, concerning his justification.[42]

William Tyndale

Both Joye and Barnes, who in earlier days had been fellow members with Tyndale of the circle that used to meet at the White Horse Inn in Cambridge, renewed their associations with Tyndale during their years of exile on the Continent, whither he had betaken himself in 1524 so that he might fulfil the task of translating the Scriptures into English; and both Joye and Barnes must have been familiar with Tyndale's work *The Parable of the Wicked Mammon*, essentially a treatise on the theme of justification by faith, which was published in 1528, the year of their escape to Europe. Their own works on justification did not appear until 1531, as we have noticed. Tyndale in his composition freely used material from a sermon preached by Luther in 1522, and it was in particular through him and Barnes, largely as a result of their personal associations with the German reformer, that elements of Luther's thought filtered through into the Anglican mind. There would in fact prove to be an essential harmony or consensus of judgment between Geneva, Canterbury and Wittenberg regarding the doctrine of justification. It was Luther's contentious eucharistic teaching which Calvin and Cranmer were never able to accept.

The Augsburg Confession of 1530, which Melanchthon had prepared and Luther had approved, also contained a clear formulation on the subject of justification, affirming that

> we cannot obtain forgiveness of sin and righteousness before God by our own merits, works, or satisfactions, but we receive forgiveness of sin and become righteous before God by grace, for Christ's sake, through faith, when we believe that Christ suffered for us and that for his sake our sin is forgiven and righteousness and eternal life are given to us; for God will regard and reckon this faith as righteousness, as Paul says in Romans 3:21-26 and 4:5 (Article IV).

Another paragraph explained the Lutheran understanding of the importance of good works as follows:

> It is also taught among us that such faith should produce good fruits and good works and that we must do all such good works as God commanded, but we should do them for God's sake and not place our trust in them as if thereby to merit favor before God. For we receive forgiveness of sin and righteousness through faith in Christ, as Christ himself says, 'So you also, when you have done all that is commanded you, say, We are unworthy servants' (Luke 17:10). The Fathers also teach thus, for Ambrose says, 'It is ordained of God that whoever believes in Christ shall be saved, and he shall have forgiveness of sins, not through works but through faith alone, without merit' (Article VI).[43]

These statements on faith, works and justification were thoroughly congenial to Tyndale and to the Anglican understanding that was being shaped during the thirties and forties of this century and would find official expression in the Articles of Religion, the Homilies, and *The Book of Common Prayer*. In his *Parable of the Wicked Mammon* Tyndale maintained that "faith only before all works and without all merits, but Christ's only, justifieth and setteth us at peace with God."[44] Just as a man "that hath his feet in fetters, gives, or stocks must first be loosed ere he can go, walk, or run," so also the bonds of sin must first be removed before a person is able to do works pleasing to God:

> This is therefore plain, and a sure conclusion, not to be doubted of, that there must be first in the heart of a man, before he do any good work, a greater and a preciouser thing than all the good works in the world, to reconcile him to God, to bring the love and favour of God to him, to make him love God again, to make him righteous and good in the sight of God, to do away his sin, to deliver him and loose him out of that captivity wherein he was conceived and born, in which he could neither love God nor the will of God. . . . That precious thing which must be in the heart ere a man can work any good is the word of God, which in the Gospel preacheth, proffereth, and bringeth unto all that repent and believe the favour of God in Christ. Whosoever heareth the word and believeth it, the same is thereby righteous; and thereby is given him the Spirit of God, which leadeth him unto all that is the will of God; and is loosed from the captivity and bondage of the devil; and his heart is free to love God, and hath lust to do the will of God.[45]

Even this saving faith in the Gospel is not something generated by man but God's gift, freely bestowed. In asserting that "it is altogether the pure gift of God poured into us freely, without all manner of doing of us, without deserving and merits, yea, and without seeking for of us, and is even God's gift and grace, purchased through Christ," Tyndale cites the support of Ephesians 2:8f., were St. Paul declares, "By grace you have been saved through faith, and this is not your own doing, it is the gift of God — not because of works, lest any man should boast."[46] And, again, the right faith must be expected to bring forth good works; for, "as the fruit maketh not the tree good, but declareth and testifieth outwardly that the tree is good, . . . even so shall ye know the right faith by her fruit."[47] At the conclusion of this work, where he writes that "faith justifieth us not, that is to say, marrieth us not to God, that we should continue unfruitful as before, but that he should put the seed of his Holy Spirit in us (as St. John in his first epistle calleth it)[48] and make us fruitful," Tyndale quotes not only Ephesians 2:8 and 9 but also verse 10, which immediately adds: "For we are his workmanship, created in Christ Jesus unto good works, which God hath ordained that we should walk in them."[49] It is on the basis of this apostolic teaching that he is able to state: "We are sure therefore that God hath created and made us new in Christ, and put his Spirit in us, that we should live a new life, which is the life of good works."[50]

To the question, "What shall we say then to those scriptures which sound as though a man should do good works, and live well, for heaven's sake or eternal reward?," Tyndale replies that is in Christ and not at all because of his own achievements that the believer inherits all things.

So now thou seest that life eternal and all good things are promised unto faith and belief, so that he that believeth on Christ shall be safe. Christ's blood hath purchased life for us, and hath made us the heirs of God, so that heaven cometh by Christ's blood. If thou wouldest obtain heaven with the merits and deservings of thine own works, so didst thou wrong, yea, and shamedst, the blood of Christ, and unto thee were Christ dead in vain. Now is the true believer heir of God by Christ's deservings; yea, and in Christ was predestinate and ordained unto eternal life before the world began. And when the Gospel is preached unto us we believe the mercy of God, and in believing we receive the Spirit of God, which is the earnest of eternal life, and we are in eternal life already, and feel already in our hearts the sweetness thereof, and are overcome with the kindness of God and Christ; and therefore love the will of God, and of love are ready to work freely, and not to obtain that which is given to us freely and whereof we are heirs already.

Accordingly, he admonishes the believer: "Let thine eye be single, and look unto good living only, and take no thought for the reward, but be content; forasmuch as thou knowest and art sure . . . that thou art heir of all the goodness of God, and that all good things are thine already, purchased by Christ's blood."[51] To ascribe to the deserving of one's own works that which is freely given by the merits of Christ's blood is to rob Christ of his honor.[52] Tyndale insists, indeed, that "God's honour is the final end of all good works."[53]

Tyndale's celebrated *Prologue upon the Epistle to the Romans*, which was published in 1526, is for the most part a reproduction of Luther's Preface to that Epistle; but in the concluding pages he gives his own explanation not only of the purpose of the Epistle but also of the doctrine of justification in the New Testament. The passage is worthy of extensive quotation:

> The sum and whole cause of the writing of this epistle is to prove that a man is justified by faith only; which proposition whoso denieth to him is not only this epistle and all that Paul writeth, but also the whole Scripture, so locked up, that he shall never understand it to his soul's health. And, to bring a man to the understanding and feeling that faith only justifieth, Paul proves that the whole nature of man is so poisoned and so corrupt, yea, and so dead, concerning godly living or godly thinking, that it is impossible for her to keep the law in the sight of God; that is to say, to love it, and of love and willingness to do it as naturally as a man eats or drinks, until he be quickened again and healed through faith.
>
> And by justifying understand no other thing than to be reconciled to God, and to be restored unto his favour, and to have thy sins forgiven thee. And when I say God justifieth us, understand thereby that God, for Christ's sake, merits, and deservings only, receiveth us unto his mercy, favour, and grace, and forgiveth us our sins. And when I say Christ justifieth us, understand thereby that Christ only hath redeemed us, bought, and delivered us out of the wrath of God and damnation, and hath with his works only purchased us the mercy, the favour, and grace of God, and the forgiveness of our sins. And when I say that faith justifieth, understand thereby that faith and trust in the truth of

God and in the mercy promised us for Christ's sake, and for his deserving and works only, doth quiet the conscience and certify her that our sins be forgiven, and we in the favour of God.
Furthermore, set before thine eyes Christ's works and thine works. Christ's works only justify thee and make satisfaction for thy sin, and not thine own works
. . . . For the promise is made thee for Christ's work's sake, and not for thine own work's sake. . . .
Finally, that we say faith only justifieth ought to offend no man. For if this be true, that Christ only redeemed us, Christ only bare our sins, made satisfaction for them, and purchased us the favour of God, then must it needs be true that the trust only in Christ's deserving and in the promises of God the Father, made to us for Christ's sake, doth alone quiet the conscience and certify it that the sins are forgiven.[54]

Thomas Cranmer

The strength of this dynamic theological surge was increasingly making itself felt in England when, in 1532, Thomas Cranmer was appointed Archbishop of Canterbury by Henry VIII. The English king, despite his conflict with the Pope over his matrimonial problems and his political maneuverings with civil and ecclesiastical promoters of reform in Germany, remained a Catholic to his dying day. But, even so, he held Philip Melanchthon in high respect and made several attempts to bring him over to England.[55] Henry also evinced a considerable degree of sympathy for the definitions of the Augsburg Confession, of which, as we have mentioned, Melanchton was the primary author. 1536 saw the promulgation of the *Ten Articles*, "Devised by the King's Highness Majesty to establish Christian quietness and unity among us and to avoid contentious opinions." These articles reflect no doubt a measure of political expediency on the king's part, but also the transitional character of the theology in England at that time. They represent an endeavor to accommodate Anglican teaching to that of the Augsburg Confession, though only to a certain degree, for they offer an uneasy mixture of both reformed and unreformed notions.
The fifth of these Ten Articles explained justification as signifying "the remission of sins and acceptance into the

favour of God, that is to say, a perfect renovation in Christ"; and "contrition, faith, and charity" were declared "both to concur in and to follow" the attaining of justification. More explicit was the affirmation of the third article on penance (which Luther still retained as a sacrament) that to contrition "must be joined a faith of the mercy and goodness of God, whereby the penitent must hope that God will forgive him and repute him justified and of the number of his elect children, not for the worthiness of any merit or work done by him, but for the only merits of the blood and passion of our Saviour Jesus Christ." The requirement was added that the people should be instructed that, "though God pardoned sin only for the satisfaction of Christ, yet they must bring forth the fruits of penance, prayer, fasting, alms-deeds, with restitution and satisfaction for wrongs done to others, with other works of mercy and charity, and obedience to God's commandments."[56]

A couple of years later, in 1538, Cranmer and two other bishops drew up in consultation with three German theologians, who had come to England as Lutheran representatives, *Thirteen Articles* in which the influence of the Augsburg Confession was still more strongly shown. For reasons which need not be discussed here these articles did not receive official sanction and in fact remained undiscovered among Cranmer's papers for more than three hundred years. Their significance lies in the evidence they provide that Cranmer's mind was advancing in a reforming direction which would subsequently lead on to the composition of the Forty-Two Articles of 1553. The royal recoil from the negotiations with the German protestants was signalized by the passage of the *Six Articles* in 1539 in which, despite Cranmer's pleas to the contrary, the gains in the direction of reform were virtually annulled (apart from the requirement of the fourth article that clergy should honor their vows of chastity). Hugh Latimer and Nicholas Shaxton, embarrassed by this reverse, resigned their respective bishoprics of Worcester and Salisbury and were thrown into prison. Henry's good will and confidence towards Cranmer continued unchanged, however, and it was actually in response to the king's request that Cranmer set down in writing the reasons, buttressed by biblical and patristic quotations, for his disapproval of the *Six Articles.*

Cranmer was a gentle person by nature, but he had never been slow to speak out boldy in the presence of the king where matters of faith were at issue. Burnet recounts how some half dozen years previously, that is to say, only a year or so after his consecration as archbishop, Cranmer, when conversing with the king, "represented to him that since he had put down the pope's authority it was not fit to let those doctrines be still taught which had no other foundation but the decrees of popes," and "pressed the king to give order to hear and examine things freely, that, when the pope's power was rejected, the people might not be obliged to believe doctrines which had no better warrant." Subsequently, in a speech before the House of Lords, he expressed the following judgment (as summarized by Burnet):

> He had much doubting in himself as to general councils,[57] and he thought that only the word of God was the rule of faith, which ought to take place in all controversies of religion. The Scriptures were called canonical as being the only rules of the faith of Christians, and these, by appointment of the ancient councils, were only to be read in the churches. The fathers SS. Ambrose, Jerome and Augustine did in many things differ from one another, but always appealed to the Scriptures as the common and certain standard. And he cited some remarkable passage out of St. Augustine to show what difference he put between the Scriptures and all the other writings, even of the best and holiest fathers.[58]

The Homilies of the Church of England

That Cranmer did not relax his efforts to re-establish the Church of England on the foundation of biblical doctrine and morality is shown, amongst other things, by his preparation of a book of homilies, which was designed not only as an antidote for the incompetence of so many of the clergy as preachers but also as a means of reaching the people with instruction that was scriptural and free from superstition. The project was proposed and approved at the meeting of Convocation in January 1542, with the intention of "making such a stay of errors as were then by ignorant preachers spread among the people."[59] Cranmer lost no time in the prosecution of this objective which he considered to be of such importance for the healing of the Church's ills — though the reading of homilies was never meant to be a substitute for preaching but a temporary or interim measure, rather, until such time as an adequate number of able preachers should be available. In February of the following year a set of homiles "composed by certain prelates of divers matters" was produced and handed over to Convocation; but the publication of these homilies was blocked, presumably by the king's decision, and it was only after the death of Henry VIII, more than four years later, that it became possible to to bring them out.[60]

The twelve homiles which were published together at the end of July 1547, now known as the *First Book of Homilies* (as distinct from the *Second Book of Homilies* brought out under Elizabeth I), contained contributions by Cranmer on "The Salvation of Mankind by only Christ our Saviour from Sin and Death Everlasting" (No. 3, the text of which is given below, pp. 49ff.), "The True, Lively, and Christian Faith" (No. 4), "Good Works annexed unto Faith" (No. 5), and also "A Fruitful Exhortation to the Reading and Knowledge of Holy Scripture" (No. 1).[61] There are, however, two components of the Second or Elizabethan Book of Homilies which actually date back to a time before 1542, namely, the "Homily for Good Friday, concerning the Death and Passion of our Saviour Jesus Christ" (which is divided into two parts) and the "Homily of the Resurrection of our Saviour Jesus Christ" for Easter Day, both of which were originally published in 1540 in the volume of *Postils on the Epistles and Gospels* edited by Richard Taverner.[62] There is some probability that they are a revision and an extension by Taverner of postils first written by Miles Coverdale;[63] but, be that as it may, the two homilies mentioned are of interest here because of the teaching they give that bears on the theme of justification.

The Good Friday homily exhorts the hearer to remember "this excellent act and benefit of Christ's death, whereby he hath purchased for us the undoubted pardon and forgiveness of our sins," and that he did so by "putting himself between God's deserved wrath and our sin." When we consider "the grievous debt of sin which could none otherwise be paid but by the death of an innocent" it is obvious that "no man can love sin, which God hateth so much, and be in his favour." Indeed, our hatred of sin should correspond to our love to God: "So much do we love God and Christ as we hate sin. . . . For Christ hath not so redeemed us from sin that we may safely return thereto again." The atoning death of Christ is the sole ground of our justification before God:

> No tongue surely is able to express the worthiness of this so precious a death. For in this standeth the continual pardon of our daily offences, in this resteth our justification, in this we be allowed, in this is purchased the everlasting health of all our souls; yea, there is none other thing that can be named under heaven to save our souls[64] but this only work of Christ's precious offering of his body upon the altar of the cross.[65]

An eloquent appeal is made to the hearer to respond to the totally undeserved grace and mercy of God freely offered to all who repent and believe:

> But O the abundant riches of God's great mercy! O the unspeakable goodness of his heavenly wisdom! When all hope of righteousness was past on our part, when we had nothing in ourselves whereby we might quench his burning wrath, and work the salvation of our own souls, and rise out of the miserable estate wherein we lay, then, even then, did Christ the Son of God, by the appointment of his Father, come down from heaven to be wounded for our sakes, to be reputed with the wicked, to be condemned unto death, to take upon him the reward of our sins, and to give his body to be broken on the cross for our offences.[66] . . . O that we should be the occasion of his death and the only cause of his condemnation! . . . O my brethren, let this image of Christ crucified be always printed in our hearts; let it stir us up to the hatred of sin and provoke our minds to the earnest love of God![67]

But the hearers are admonished that "the death of Christ shall stand us in no force, unless we apply it to ourselves in such sort as God hath appointed" — for God has decreed "a certain mean" by which we may appropriate its benefit: "What mean is that? Forsooth it is faith." Citing the assur-

ance of John 3:16 that whosoever believes in Christ will not
perish but have life everlasting, the homilist proceeds:

> Here is the mean whereby we must apply the fruits of
> Christ's death unto our deadly wound; here is the
> mean whereby we must obtain eternal life: namely,
> faith.

And, after quoting further passages from the New Testament, this lesson is pressed home as follows:

> The only mean and instrument of salvation required of
> our parts is faith, that is to say, a sure trust and con-
> fidence in the mercies of God, whereby we persuade
> ourselves that God both hath and will forgive our sins,
> that he hath accepted us again into his favour, that he
> hath released us from the bonds of damnation, and
> received us again into the number of his elect people,
> not for our merits and deserts, but only and solely for
> the merits of Christ's death and passion, who became
> man for our sakes, and humbled himself to sustain the
> reproach of the cross, that we thereby might be saved
> and made inheritors of the kingdom of heaven."[68]

The Easter homily expounds further the significance for
the Christian of the death and resurrection of Jesus:

> By his death hath he wrought for us this victory, and by
> his resurrection hath he purchased everlasting life
> and righteousness for us . . . He passed through death
> and hell to the intent to put us in good hope that by his
> strength we shall do the same. He paid the ransom of
> sin, that it should not be laid to our charge.[69]

In the preceding homily on the Passion the congregation
was reminded that the purpose of "being washed in our baptism from the filthiness of sin" is "that we should live afterward in the pureness of life";[70] and here again they are ex-
horted to make the symbolism of death-burial-resurrection
in the baptismal rite a daily reality by "rising daily from sin
to righteousness and holiness of life" and living selflessly
"to the honouring of God and the profiting of your neigh-
bour."[71] Works, once more, follow faith. There is not intention to exclude them or to minimize their importance in the

life of the person who is justified. But they come after, not before justification: as they are the fruit so also they are the evidence of genuine faith.

The foregoing survey of some of the main stages in the reformulation of the doctrine of Christian justification provides the background against which a proper understanding may be gained both of Cranmer's statements on the subject in homilies and articles and also, in large measure, of the definition propounded by Hooker in the latter part of the same century.

The Homily on Salvation

The third homily in the Edwardian book is a careful exposition of the New Testament teaching concerning justification. It displays the settled judgment at which Cranmer had arrived on this important issue by the year 1547. From the opening affirmation of the universal sinfulness of mankind he draws the conclusion that "therefore can no man by his own acts, works, and deeds, seem they never so good, be justified and made righteous before God." Accordingly, "another righteousness or justification" must be sought, which comes not from man but from God, that, namely, "which we receive by God's mercies and Christ's merits" and which, "embraced by faith, is taken, accepted, and allowed of God for our perfect and full justification." The believer's justification rests upon the double foundation, firstly, of the perfection of Christ's life as he faultlessly fulfilled the will of God, and, secondly, the satisfaction made for our sins by Christ when he suffered and died, the innocent for the guilty, on the cross. The ransom provided by God for us was that of "the most precious body and blood of his own most dear and best beloved Son Jesus Christ" who had "fulfilled the law for us perfectly." It was in this way that "the justice of God and his mercy did embrace together and fulfilled the mystery of our redemption."[72]

Three passages are cited from the Epistle to the Romans[73] to show that there are "three things which must go together in our justification":

upon God's part, his great mercy and grace; upon Christ's part, justice, that is, the satisfaction of God's

justice, or the price of our redemption by the offering
of his body and shedding of his blood with fulfilling of
the law perfectly and throughly; and upon our part,
true and lively faith in the merits of Jesus Christ, which
yet is not ours but by God's working in us.[74]

It is evident, then, that "the grace of God doth not shut out
the justice of God in our justification, but only shutteth out
the justice of man, that is to say, the justice of our works, as
to be merits of deserving or justification"; and Cranmer is
able confidently to affirm that "Christ is now the righteousness of all that truly do believe in him," precisely because
"he for them paid their ransom by his death" and "he for
them fulfilled the law in his life."[75]

After drawing attention to numerous other New Testament
passages, Cranmer calls in the testimony of the Church's
patristic authors. "After this wise to be justified, only by
this true and lively faith in Christ," he asserts, "speak all the
old and ancient authors, both Greek and Latins"; and, having given quotations from Hilary, Basil and Ambrose, he
mentions also Origen, Chrysostom, Cyprian, Augustine,
Prosper, Ecumenius, Photius, Bernard, Anselm, "and many
other authors." This leads him to state confidently:

> This faith the Holy Scripture teacheth; this is the strong
> rock and foundation of Christian religion; this doctrine
> all old and ancient authors of Christ's Church do ap-
> prove; this doctrine advanceth and setteth forth the
> true glory of Christ, and beateth down the vain glory of
> man; this whosoever denieth is not to be counted for a
> true Christian man nor for a setter forth of Christ's
> glory, but for an adversary of Christ and his Gospel,
> and for a setter forth of men's vainglory.[76]

At the same time Cranmer is careful to explain that justification by faith alone does not imply the exclusion of good
works from the Christian life. This saving faith, he says,
"doth not shut out repentance, hope, love, dread, and the
fear of God, to be joined with faith in every man that is
justified, but it shutteth them out from the office of justifying"; indeed, it is beyond question that "we are most
bounden to serve God in doing good deeds commanded by
him in his Holy Scripture all the days of our life."[77] No more

did the patristic writers, in teaching this doctrine, mean that "we should or might afterward be idle" or that "we should do no good works at all"; their intention, simply, was "to take away clearly all merit of our works, as being unable to deserve our justification at God's hands."[78] For anyone to profess to be a believer and Christ's disciple "when he liveth ungodly and denieth Christ in his deeds" is a dreadful contradiction. It can only be concluded that a professed faith "which bringeth forth, without repentance, either evil works or no good works is not a right, pure, and lively faith, but a dead, devilish, counterfeit, and feigned faith, as St. Paul and St. James call it."[79]

It must not be imagined, however, that genuine, lively faith is itself the ground of justification or a kind of act deserving of salvation. Such faith is our response to the grace of God freely offered us in Christ. It is the opposite and the end of self-reliance; for "it putteth us from itself, and remitteth or appointeth us unto Christ, for to have only by him remission of sins or justification." It is, Cranmer points out, as though our very faith in Christ says to us: "It is not I that take away your sins, but it is Christ only; and to him only I send you for that purpose, forsaking therein all your good virtues, words, thoughts, and works, and only putting your trust in Christ."[80]

This homily belongs in a special way to the official teaching of the Church of England, for it not only has a place in the *First Book of Homilies* which was authorized for use in the parishes under both Edward and Elizabeth, but it is also particularly referred to in the Articles of Religion as the accepted declaration of the doctrine of justification. This reference is found in the eleventh of the Forty-Two Articles of 1553, which then was limited to the brief statement:

> Justification by only faith in Jesus Christ, in the sense as is declared in the Homily of Justification, is a most certain and wholesome doctrine for Christian men.

It was in 1571 that the Articles were finally shaped and sanctioned as the Thirty-Nine Articles of the Church of England; but Article 11 was expanded to the form in which it has come down to us in the earlier Elizabethan recension of 1563, to read as follows:

We are accounted righteous before God only for the
merit of our Lord and Saviour Jesus Christ, by faith,
and not for our own works or deservings. Wherefore
that we are justified by faith only is a most wholesome
doctrine and very full of comfort, as more largely is expressed in the Homily of Justification.[81]

The Articles of Religion

Articles 10 to 14 of the Thirty-Nine, which treat respectively of Free Will, the Justification of Man, Good Works,
Works before Justification, and Works of Supererogation,
are still not free from misunderstanding in some quarters.
The key to their interpretation is the recognition that they
all make affirmations which relate specifically to the sinner's inability to justify himself before God. Their concern is
not with what is sometimes called civil righteousness; for
they are not intended to deny that even in the society of
unbelievers there are degrees of morality — that it is good
for a person to be honest and compassionate and bad for
him to be violent and dishonorable, that there is a distinction between good citizens and bad citizens, and between
good government and bad government. Their concern,
rather, is with the relationship between man and his
Creator, to whom he is ultimately accountable[82] (though of
course the nature of one's relationship with God cannot fail
to affect the nature of one's relationship with fellow human
beings). The scene is really set in Article 9, on Original Sin,
which asserts that in his state of fallenness "man is very far
gone from original righteousness and is of his own nature in-
clined to evil." This teaching strikes not only at pelagianism
(mentioned in the first part of the article), which affirms the
natural ability of man on his own, but also at the semipela-
gian affirmation of man's natural ability to cooperate with
God's grace for the achievement of justification which had
become entrenched in the theology of the Roman Catholic
Church.

This insistence on the incompetence of unregenerate
man to effect or contribute to his own justification is more
fully expressed in Article 10, which reads as follows:

The condition of man after the fall of Adam is such that
he cannot turn and prepare himself by his own natural

strength and good works to faith and calling upon God. Wherefore we have no power to do good works pleasant and acceptable to God without the grace of God by Christ preventing us, that we may have a good will, and working with us when we have that good will.

The declaration of this article, which, in its first part, is indebted to the Württemberg Confession and, in its latter part, to Augustine's treatise on Grace and Free Will,[83] that fallen man is unable not merely to do but even to will what is pleasing to God is based on the apostolic teaching that prior to and apart from the divine work of regeneration man is dead through his sins, and therefore incapable of contributing to his salvation; once brought to life through faith in Christ, however, he is "created in Christ Jesus for good works which God prepared beforehand for us to walk in," and, further, he experiences the reality that "God is at work in him, both to will and to work for his good pleasure."[84]

There is an essential distinction, then, between the sinner's justification, which is entirely due to the prevenient grace of God, and the believer's sanctification, his growth in holiness or Christ-likeness, which is being effected in cooperation with the grace of God. Justification is a status, instananeous and total, as the perfect righteousness of Christ is applied or imputed to believers on the ground of his atoning death which paid the penalty of man's unrighteousness. Sanctification is a process whereby the believer, constantly aided by the inward working of the Holy Spirit, is progressively being transformed as he advances towards the goal of Christ's perfection[85] — a goal reached not here and now but hereafter at Christ's appearing.[86] But the Articles are emphatic in their insistence that the good works of sanctification contribute in no way to man's justification. As Article 11 says, it is "not for our own works or deservings" that "we are accounted righteous before God," but "only for the merit of our Lord and Saviour Jesus Christ by faith"; and the fact that "we are justified by faith only" is described as "a most wholesome doctrine and very full of comfort" because the accounting of the righteousness of Christ to the believer can only mean justification that is final and complete, whereas justification that depends on ourselves, whether entirely or partially, can only, because of our imperfection, leave us in a state of uncertainty and insecurity.

The clear distinction between justification and sanctification is brought out in Article 12 (which was added in 1563). There we read that "good works, which are the fruits of faith and follow after justification" — in other words, which belong to sanctification — "are pleasing and acceptable to God in Christ," indeed that they "spring out necessarily of a true and lively faith" and are themselves the evidence of that faith, "insomuch that by them a lively faith may be as evidently known as a tree discerned by the fruit." But it is carefully explained that these good works "cannot put away our sins and endure the severity of God's judgment" — that is to say, sanctification must not be confused with justification; otherwise even the good works of sanctification will, because of their imperfection, lead to condemnation rather than justification. This understanding of the human situation rests on the teaching of the New Testament that, as Article 15 affirms, Christ alone is without sin;[87] whereas, contrariwise, "all we the rest, although baptized and born again in Christ, yet offend in many things," with the consequence that "if we say we have no sin we deceive ourselves and the truth is not in us."[88]

If works done after justification cannot put away our sins, no more, as Article 13 teaches, can "works done before the grace of Christ and the inspiration of the Spirit." The former, we have been assured, are pleasing to God;[89] but we are admonished that the latter "are not pleasant to God, forasmuch as they spring not of faith in Jesus Christ." The opinion of the medieval "school authors" is rejected, that works before justification "make men meet to receive grace or deserve grace of congruity," since such works "are not done as God hath willed and commanded them to be done." The further medieval notion of supererogation, which, with its concept of the achievement of an excess of merit by the great saints (confusing justification and sanctification once again), lay behind the contemporary trade in indulgences, is condemned in Article 14. This article warns that works of supererogation, defined as "voluntary works besides, over, and above God's commandments," by which it is supposed that men "do not only render unto God as much as they are bound to do, but that they do more for his sake than of bounden duty is required," are something that "cannot be taught without arrogancy and impiety." Sufficient support for this conclusion is found in Christ's plain statement: "When ye have done all that are commanded of you, say, We are unprofitable servants."[90]

John Jewel

When a young man at Oxford, John Jewel had been an eager disciple of the Italian scholar Peter Martyr Vermigli, whom Edward VI, at the instigation of Cranmer, had appointed Regius Professor of Divinity in that university. The close relationship was renewed when, during the reign of Mary, Jewel found refuge on the Continent. With the accession of Elizabeth, in 1558, and his return to England, Jewel was the queen's choice for the bishopric of Salisbury, and his intellectual brilliance assured him of an undisputed place in the forefront of Anglican scholarship. He had also enjoyed the trust and friendship of Archbishop Cranmer, and even after the latter's arrest had served as one of his two notaries, making a *verbatim* record of the disputation in Oxford that preceded his burning.[91] Thus, like the other leaders whom Elizabeth appointed to high ecclesiastical office, Jewel had firm and early roots in the soil of Cranmerian reform.

Jewel's was an extremely productive pen, but the most celebrated of all his works is the *Apology of the Church of England* which was published, in Latin, in 1562. It was the derogatory judgments and anathemas pronounced against the Elizabethan Church by the Council of Trent, then nearing its conclusion (it had been in session on and off since 1545), that made such a defence or *apologia* a necessity. Ever since its first appearance Jewel's treatise has been accepted as a classical statement of the Anglican position. As John Booty has said, "the evidence which the work provides of the ecumenical character of English theology in the first part of the Elizabethan period" is "of great importance," and those who read the *Apology* "will make contact with the spirit of the Reformation in a general sense, realizing that Jewel, like Cranmer, believed that the bonds uniting the reformers were stronger and far more important than the issues which separated them."[92] Jewel proposed to "show it

plain" to the Tridentine critics "that God's holy Gospel, the
ancient bishops, and the primitive church do make on our
side, and that we have not without just cause left these
men, and rather have returned to the apostles and old
catholic fathers."[93]

In response to the charge of heresy, Jewel makes his appeal to the doctrine of Scripture as the authentic arbiter
between the false and the true:

Nowadays the Holy Scripture is abroad, the writings of
the apostles and prophets are in print, whereby all
truth and catholic doctrine may be proved, and all
heresy may be disproved and confuted. Since, then,
they bring forth none of these for themselves, and call
us nevertheless heretics, who have neither fallen from
Christ, nor from the apostles, nor yet from the prophets,
this is an injurious and very spiteful dealing. With this
sword did Christ put off the devil when he was tempted
of him. With these weapons ought all presumption,
which doth advance itself against God, to be overthrown and conquered. 'For all Scripture,' saith St.
Paul, 'that cometh by the inspiration of God, is profitable to teach, to confute, to instruct, and to reprove;
that the man of God may be perfect and throughly
framed to every good work.'[94] Thus did the holy fathers
alway fight against the heretics with none other force
than with the Holy Scriptures. . . . For at that time
made the catholic fathers and bishops no doubt but
that our religion might be proved out of the Holy Scriptures. Neither were they ever so hardy to take any for
an heretic whose error they could not evidently and apparently reprove by the selfsame Scriptures.[95]

As for the question of the sinner's justification before
God, not only does Jewel object to the "innumerable sorts
of mediators, and that utterly without the authority of
God's Word," accumulated in the unreformed church, but
he also asserts the unique mediatorship of Christ: "Neither
have we any other mediator and intercessor, by whom we
may have access to God the Father, than Jesus Christ, in
whose only name all things are obtained at his Father's
hand."[96] And the unique mediatorship of Christ is itself
centered on the everlasting perfection of his unique offer-

ing of himself, the incarnate Son, in the sinner's stead. Jewel explains this is in the following manner:

> We say, also, that every person is born in sin and leadeth his life in sin; that nobody is able truly to say his heart is clean; that the most righteous person is but an unprofitable servant; that the law of God is perfect and requireth of us perfect and full obedience; that we are able by no means to fulfil that law in this worldly life; that there is no one mortal creature who can be justified by his own deserts in God's sight; and therefore that our only succour and refuge is to fly to the mercy of our Father by Jesu Christ, and assuredly to persuade our minds that he is the obtainer of forgiveness for our sins, and that by his blood all our spots of sin be washed clean.[97]

Again, however, the insistence on the justification of the sinner by faith alone, to the exclusion of all supposedly meritorious works apart from the perfect atoning work of Christ, was in no way intended to imply that the performance of good works was of no importance in the life of the Christian; for, as we have seen, true faith must be expected to be productive of works that are pleasing to God. Thus Jewel affirms:

> Though we say that we have no meed at all by our own works and deeds, but appoint all the mean of our salvation to be in Christ alone, yet say we not that for this cause men ought to live loosely and dissolutely, nor that is enough for a Christian to be baptized only and to believe, as though there were nothing else required at his hand. For true faith is lively, and can in no wise be idle. Thus therefore teach we the people that God hath called us, not to follow riot and wantonness, but, as Paul saith, 'unto good works, to walk in them'; that God plucked us out 'from the power of darkness, to serve the living God,' to cut away all the remnants of sin and 'to work our salvation in fear and trembling'; that it may appear how that the Spirit of sanctification is in our bodies and that Christ himself doth dwell in our hearts.[98]

Jewel's *Defence* of his *Apology* against the criticisms of Thomas Harding is distinguished not only by his comprehensive knowledge of Holy Scripture but also by an overwhelming display of patristic learning, which testifies impressively to the amazing range of his erudition. When, for example, Harding objected that the expression "faith alone" (*sola fides*) was not used by St. Paul, Jewel retorted that 'when St. Paul excludeth all manner of works besides only faith' — as in the assertions, 'we be justified freely of his grace, we judge that a man is justified by faith, without the works of the law, we know that a man is not justified by the works of the law, but by the faith of Christ' [99] — 'what else then leaveth he but faith alone?' And thereupon he continues: 'Howbeit, if it be so horrible an heresy to say we be justified before God by only faith, that is to say, only by the merits and cross of Christ, let us see what the holy learned fathers of the Church so many hundred years ago have taught us thereof'; and he proceeds to summon as supporting witnesses Ambrose ('They are justified freely, because, working nothing, and requiting nothing, they are justified by only faith through the gift of God'; 'This was God's determination, that, the law surceasing, the grace of God should require only faith unto salvation'; and, 'Only faith is laid or appointed unto salvation'), Basil ('He knoweth himself to be void of true righteousness and to be justified by only faith in Christ'), Theodoret ('Not by any works of ours, but by only faith we have gotten the mystical good things'), Gregory of Nazianzus ('Only believing is righteousness'), Origen ('Where is now thy boasting? It is shut out. Paul saith that the justification of only faith is sufficient, so that a man only believing may be justified, although he have done no good works at all'), Hesychius ('The grace of God is given only of mercy and favour, and is embraced and received by only faith'), and Chrysostom ('They said, Whoso stayeth himself by only faith is accursed; contrariwise St. Paul proveth that whoso stayeth himself by only faith, he is blessed') — all of whom approve and employ the expression 'only faith' (*sola fides*).[100]

Richard Hooker

Jewel's protégé and disciple Richard Hooker maintained and promoted the same teaching his master had so ably expounded. It is Hooker who, in classical manner, concludes

the line and confirms the position of the reformed Anglicanism of the sixteenth century. There are, indeed, echoes of
Jewel in his definitions of the doctrine of justification by
faith alone. Thus in the second of two sermons on Jude
17-21 we find him explaining, with reference to the exhortation to 'build up ourselves in our most holy faith':

> No, it is not the worthiness of our believing, it is the virtue
> of him in whom we believe, by which we stand sure, as
> houses that are builded upon a rock. He is a wise man
> who hath builded his house upon a rock; for he hath
> chosen a good foundation, and no doubt his house will
> stand. But how shall it stand? Verily, by the strength of
> the rock which beareth it, and by nothing else . . . So
> that every heart must this think, and every tongue
> must thus speak, 'Not unto us, O Lord, not unto us', nor
> unto any thing which is within us, but unto thy name
> only, only to thy name belongeth all the praise of all
> the treasures and riches of every temple which is of
> God. This excludeth all boasting and vaunting of our
> faith.[101]

Hooker denounces the notion that any man can by his own
meritorious works justify himself before God, let alone accumulate a surplus of personal merit (through works of
supererogation) which can then be made available to
others, and insists on the *imputation* of the perfect righteousness of Christ to the unworthy but believing sinner as
the only means of our justification before God:

> A strange and a strong delusion it is wherewith the
> Man of Sin hath bewitched the world, a forcible spirit of
> error it must needs be, which hath brought men to
> such a senseless and unreasonable persuasion as this
> is, not only that men clothed with mortality and sin, as
> we ourselves are, can do God so much service as shall
> be able to make a full and perfect satisfaction before
> the tribunal seat of God for their own sins, yea a great
> deal more than is sufficient for themselves, but also
> that a man at the hands of a bishop or a pope, for such
> and such a price, may buy the overplus of other men's
> merits, purchase the fruits of other men's labours, and
> build his soul by another man's faith . . . Our faith
> being such, is that indeed which St. Jude doth here

term faith: namely, a thing most *holy*. The reason is
this: we are justified by faith; for Abraham believed,
and this was imputed to him for righteousness.[102]
Being justified, all our iniquities are covered; [103] God
beholdeth us in the righteousness which is imputed,
and not in the sins which we have committed. But imputation of righteousness hath covered the sins of
every soul who believeth; God by pardoning our sin
hath taken it away: so that now, although our trans-
gressions be multiplied above the hairs of our head,
yet, being justified, we are as free and as clear as if
there were no one spot or stain of any uncleanness in
us. For it is God that justifieth; 'and who shall lay any
thing to the charge of God's chosen?' saith the Apostle
in the eighth chapter to the Romans.[104]

Hooker makes the memorable assertion that 'to make a
wicked and a sinful man most holy through his believing is
more than to create a world of nothing.' And he exclaims:

O that our hearts were stretched out like tents, and
that the eyes of our understanding were as bright as
the sun, that we might throughly know the riches of
the glorious inheritance of saints, and what is the ex-
ceeding greatness of his power towards us, whom he
accepteth for pure, and most holy through our believing![105]

Hooker's sermon or discourse on justification, the text
of which is given below,[106] was preached in London in March
1585, about a year after his appointment as Master of the
Temple. A considerable portion of it is directly related to the
controversy with Walter Travers, the afternoon lecturer at
the Temple whose presbyterian convictions had caused
him to be passed over for the mastership. According to
Izaac Walton, Travers was an able preacher and 'a man
of competent learning, of winning behaviour, and of a
blameless life.'[107] The two men apparently held each other
in esteem and enjoyed a good relationship; but Travers
voiced his objection to certain opinions that had been expressed by Hooker in his preaching, and among them the
assertion that he did not doubt that 'God was merciful to
save thousands of our fathers living in popish supersti-

tions, inasmuch as they sinned ignorantly.' On the Sunday immediately following that on which this statement was made Hooker took pains to justify this statement, within the framework of the sermon on justification. Travers described it as a 'long speech,' and such it must have been, though the text as we now possess it must be supposed to have undergone subsequent literary expansion, for otherwise it would have taken more than three hours to deliver — an inordinate amount of time even for those spacious days. As is generally the case in the conduct of controversies, neither seems to have fully represented the arguments and qualifications of the other. The discourse before us, however, sets forth Hooker's position on issues of importance for his day and for ours; though it is hard not to feel that his defence of the controverted statement would have been improved had he presented it more briefly and at points with greater clarity. He was perhaps excessively anxious to convince others that he was far from being a Romanist.

He had, after all, quite definitely affirmed in what he had said immediately before making the disputed statement that, because the Church of Rome was so corrupted in faith and refused to be reformed, 'we are to sever ourselves from her,' and that 'the example of our fathers may not retain us in communion and fellowship with that church, under the hope that we, so continuing, might be saved as well as they.' Concerning the difference between the Church of Rome and the Church of England he is most emphatic: 'We disagree about the nature of the very essence of the medicine whereby Christ cureth our disease, about the manner of applying it, about the number and the power of the means.' He does not hesitate to say that Rome is guilty of heretical teaching regarding the justification of the sinner before God, by which, he insists, 'the very foundation of faith which they hold is plainly overthrown, and the force of the blood of Jesus Christ extinguished.'

The question whether justification is by the *imputation* of Christ's righteousness or by the *infusion* of grace Hooker perceived to be of central importance. In the Roman Catholic perspective, *infused* grace is at the same time *inherent* grace, which may be augmented by the performance of meritorious works, leading to the distinction between the 'first justification' and 'the second justification,' or diminished by the commission of venial sin, or lost as the result of mortal sin. Hooker, however, denied that we can be justified 'by any inherent quality,' because 'Christ hath merited righteousness for as many as are found in him,' while at the same time affirming that it is *by faith* that 'we are incorporated into him.' The imputation of Christ's righteousness automatically implies the non-imputation of the believer's unrighteousness. Thus Hooker assures the man who trusts in Christ for salvation that God 'putteth away his sin by not imputing it, taketh quite away the punishment due thereunto, by pardoning it, and accepteth him in Christ Jesus as perfectly righteous.' On the basis of 2 Corinthians 5:21 he is able to assure all who have placed their faith in Christ: 'Such are we in the sight of God the Father as is the very Son of God himself,' and to declare that 'we care for no knowledge in the world but this, that man hath sinned and God hath suffered, that God hath made himself the sin of men, and that men are made the righteousness of God.'

Equally to be rejected is the notion that the faith of the believer in any way merits the grace of justification. Confident that 'our doctrine is no other than that which we have learned at the feet of Christ,' Hooker explains that 'God doth justify the believing man, yet not for the worthiness of his belief, but for his worthiness who is believed.' Even the reward which God promises to him who serves faithfully after justification is 'not for any meritorious dignity which is, or can be, in the work, but through his mere mercy, by whose commandment he worketh.' Indeed, a right understanding of God's justifying mercy 'is so repugnant unto merits that to say we are saved for the worthiness of anything which is ours is to deny we are saved by grace.' Hooker's position, in short, is entirely consonant with the teaching on justification, works, faith and merit propounded by Cranmer and his colleagues and by the Elizabethan divines, as well as with that of the Continental reformers.

But what about those generations who lived and died in those days when there was a famine of evangelical preaching, when the Bible was not generally available to the people in their own language, and when worship was conducted in an uncomprehended language? Did all such persons perish in their sins because they had an inadequate or faulty understanding of the biblical doctrine of justification, or because they had been taught that good works merit the grace and favour of God? This was the issue that led Hooker into the controversy we have described. He postulated a distinction between those who partake in heresies knowing them to be heresies and those who do so without knowing them to be heresies. His contention was that 'heresy is heretically maintained by such as obstinately hold it after wholesome admonition,' while, on the other hand, in the absence of any such admonition, there were 'many partakers of the error who are not of the heresy of the Church of Rome,' that is to say, who were ignorant through no fault of their own of the apostolic doctrine of the sinner's justification before God, but who yet held the foundation of belief in Jesus Christ as the incarnate Son of God and as the source, through the cross, of redeeming grace. On the basis of these and similar considerations Hooker finds it possible to assert (with the teaching of 1 Corinthians 3:10ff. in mind) that 'as many as hold the foundation which is precious, though they hold it but weakly and as it were by a slender thread, although they frame many base and unsuitable things upon it, things that cannot abide the trial of the fire, yet shall they pass the fiery trial and be saved, who indeed have builded themselves upon the rock which is the foundation of the Church.' But persistently to reject the plain teaching of Scripture on justification and obstinately to maintain that 'we cannot be saved by Christ alone without works' is, says Hooker, directly to deny the foundation of faith: such persons 'hold it not, not so much as by a slender thread.' This, he saw, was the official position of the Church of Rome, deliberately fixed by the definitions and anathemas of the Council of Trent; and hence the necessity for separation from a communion which was determiend to continue in so radical an error.

Like his predecessors in the Church of England, Hooker insisted that good works and godly living are essential for the Christian's sanctification as the fruit and evidence of saving faith, but always with the clear understanding that 'faith is the only hand which putteth on Christ unto justification, and Christ the only garment which, being so put on, covereth the shame of our defiled natures.' In contrast to the righteousness of justification, which is imputed, the righteousness of sanctification is inherent:

'unless we work, we have it not.' Hooker is careful to 'distinguish it as a thing in nature different from the righteousness of justification.' Citing Romans 6:22, he states: "Ye are made free from sin and made servants unto God": this is the righteousness of justification; "Ye have your fruit in holiness"; this is the righteousness of sanctification.'

Hooker's quarrel with the Church of Rome is that they have mixed together divine grace and human merit. 'If it were not a strong deluding spirit which hath possession of their hearts, were it possible but that they should see how plainly they do herein gainsay the very ground of apostolic faith?' he asks. 'Is this that salvation by grace whereof so plentiful mention is made in the sacred Scriptures of God? Was this their meaning who first taught the world to look for salvation only by Christ? By grace, the Apostle saith, and by grace in such sort as a gift, a thing that cometh not of ourselves, not of our works, lest any man should boast.' He regards the declaration of Titus 3:5 as almost prophetically intended for the situation now confronting him: 'The Apostle, as if he had foreseen how the Church of Rome would abuse the world in time by ambiguous terms, to declare in what sense the name of grace must be taken, when we make it the cause of our salvation, saith, "He saved us according to his mercy" . . . . Grace bestoweth freely, and therefore justly requireth the glory of that which is bestowed. We deny the grace of our Lord Jesus Christ, we imbase, disannul, annihilate the benefit of his bitter passion, if we rest in those proud imaginations that life everlasting is deservedly ours, that we merit it, and that we are worthy of it.'

In some important respects the controversy between Roman Catholicism and Anglicanism, not to mention reformed Christianity in general, remains unresolved. The authoritarian supremacy of the Pope and the Mariological dogmas, for example, together with transubstantiation and its accompaniments, continue to be a wall of separation. Moreover, the Tridentine anathemas condemning distinctive teachings of the Reformers, including the doctrine that justification is by faith alone apart from works, as taught by Cranmer and reaffirmed by Hooker, seem to be inerasably decreed. But in other respects there have been significant changes, not least in our day, and the chief of these has been the action of the Second Vatican Council in setting the

Bible free for all to read and study. In a way hardly known before, Protestants and Catholics are now able to speak gently to each other and together to seek the enlightenment of Holy Scripture; and this new spirit of good will has meant that the anathemas of Trent have become an embarrassment to many Catholics. Be that as it may, there is certainly need for all the churches to submit themselves and their ways afresh to the canon of Christ's teaching as enshrined in the apostolical writings of the New Testament, especially in view of the theological and ecclesiastical confusion which now commonly and, it seems, equally prevails in the ranks of both Catholics and non-Catholics. And Episcopalians in particular, who trace their spiritual ancestry back to men like Cranmer and Hooker, will be well advised, if they wish to recover the wholeness and coherence that should rightly be theirs, to heed once more and reappropriate the instruction given by these founding fathers of their communion.

* * * * * * * * * *

Note: The texts that follow have been slightly modernized for the benefit of the contemporary reader, but without doing violence to the style and idiom of the respective authors.

II

Thomas Cranmer

*A Homily of the Salvation
of Mankind by Only Christ Our Saviour
from Sin and Death Everlasting*

Because all men be sinners and offenders against God, and breakers of his law and commandments, therefore can no man by his own acts, works, and deeds (seem they never so good) be justified and made righteous before God; but every man of necessity is constrained to seek for another righteousness or justification, to be received at God's own hands, that is to say, the forgiveness of his sins and trespasses, in such things as he hath offended. And this justification or righteousness, which we so receive of God's mercy and Christ's merits, embraced by faith, is taken, accepted, and allowed of God for our perfect and full justification. For the more full understanding hereof, it is our parts and duties ever to remember the great mercy of God, how that (all the world being wrapped in sin by breaking of the law) God sent his only Son our Saviour Christ into this world to fulfill the law for us, and, by shedding of his most precious blood, to make a sacrifice and satisfaction, or (as it may be called) amends to his Father for our sins, to assuage his wrath and indignation conceived against us for the same.

Insomuch that infants, being baptized and dying in their infancy, are by this sacrifice washed from their sins, brought to God's favour, and made his children and inheritors of his kingdom of heaven; and they who in act or deed do sin after their baptism, when they turn again to God unfeignedly, they are likewise washed by this sacrifice from all their sins, in such sort that there remaineth not any spot of sin that shall be imputed to their damnation. This is that justification or righteousness which St. Paul speaketh of when he saith: 'No man is justified by the works of the law, but freely by faith in Jesus Christ'; and again he saith: 'We believe in Jesus Christ, that we be justified freely by the faith of Christ and not by the works of the law, because that no man shall be justified by the works of the law.'[1] And although this justification be free unto us, yet it cometh not so freely unto us that there is no ransom paid therefor at all. But here may man's reason be astonished, reasoning after this fashion: if a ransom be paid for our redemption, then it is not given us freely. For a prisoner that paid his ransom is not let go freely; for if he go freely, then he goeth without ransom: for what is it else to go freely than to be set at liberty without paying of ransom?

This reason is satisfied by the great wisdom of God in this mystery of our redemption, who hath so tempered his justice and mercy together that he would neither by his justice condemn us unto the everlasting captivity of the devil and his prison of hell, remediless for ever without mercy, nor by his mercy deliver us clearly, without justice, or payment of a just ransom; but with his endless mercy he joined his most upright and equal justice. His great mercy he showed unto us in delivering us from the former captivity, without requiring of any ransom to be paid or amends to be made upon our parts, which thing by us had been impossible to be done. And whereas it lay not in us that to do, he provided a ransom for us, that was, the most precious body and blood of his own most dear and best beloved Son Jesus Christ, who, besides this ransom, fulfilled the law for us perfectly. And so the justice of God and his mercy did embrace together,[2] and fulfilled the mystery of our redemption. And of this justice and mercy of God knit together speaketh St. Paul in the third chapter to the Romans: 'All have offended and have need of the glory of God; but are justified freely by his grace, by redemption which is in Jesus Christ, whom God hath set forth to us for a reconciler and peace-maker, through faith in his blood, to show his righteousness';[3] and in the tenth chapter: 'Christ is the end of the law, unto righteousness, to every man that believeth'[4]; and in the eighth chapter: 'That which was impossible by the law, inasmuch as it was weak by the flesh, God sending his own Son in the similitude of sinful flesh, by sin damned the world in the flesh, that the righteousness of the law might be fulfilled in us, who walk not after the flesh but after the Spirit.'[5]

In these foresaid places the Apostle toucheth specially three things which must go together in our justification. Upon God's part, his great mercy and grace; upon Christ's part, justice, that is, the satisfaction of God's justice, or the price of our redemption, by the offering of his body and the shedding of his blood, with fulfilling of the law perfectly and thoroughly; and upon our part, true and lively faith in the merits of Jesus Christ, which yet is not ours, but by God's working in us: so that in our justification is not only God's mercy and grace but also his justice, which the Apostle calleth the justice of God, and it consisteth in paying our ransom and fulfilling of the law. And so the grace of God doth not shut out the justice of God in our justification, but only shutteth out the justice of man, that is to say, the justice of our works, as to be merits of deserving our justification. And therefore St. Paul declareth here nothing upon the behalf of man concerning his justification but only a true and lively faith, which nevertheless is the gift of God, and not man's only work, without God.[6]

And yet that faith doth not shut out repentance, hope, love, dread, and the fear of God, to be joined with faith in every man that is justified; but it shutteth them out from the office of justifying: so that, although they be all present together in him that is justified, yet they justify not altogether. Nor the faith also doth not shut out the justice of our good works, necessarily to be done afterwards of duty towards God (for we are most bounden to serve God in doing good deeds commanded by him in his Holy Scripture all the days of our life);[7] but it excludeth them so that we may not do them to this intent, to be made good by doing of them. For all the good works that we can do be unperfect, and therefore not able to deserve our justification. But our justification doth come freely by the mere mercy of God, and of so great and free mercy that, whereas all the world was not able of themselves to pay any part towards their ransom, it pleased our heavenly Father of his infinite mercy, without any our desert or deserving, to prepare for us the

most precious jewels of Christ's body and blood, whereby
our ransom might be fully paid, the law fulfilled, and his
justice fully satisfied. So that Christ is now the righteousness of all them that truly do believe in him. He for them
paid their ransom by his death. He for them fulfilled the law
in his life. So that now in him, and by him, every true Christian man may be called a fulfiller of the law, forasmuch as
that which their infirmity lacked Christ's justice hath
supplied.

The Second Part of the Sermon of Salvation

Ye have heard of whom all men ought to seek their justification and righteousness, and how also this righteousness
cometh unto men by Christ's death and merits. Ye heard
also how that three things are required to the obtaining of
our righteousness, that is, God's mercy, Christ's justice,
and a true and lively faith, out of the which faith springeth
good works. Also before was declared at large that no man
can be justified by his own good works, that no man ful-
filleth the law, according to the full request of the law.

And St. Paul in his epistle to the Galatians proveth the
same, saying thus: 'If there had been any law given which
could have justified, verily righteousness should have been
the law';[8] and again he saith: 'If righteousness be by the law,
then Christ died in vain;[9] and again he saith: 'You that are
justified by the law are fallen away from grace';[10] and furthermore, he writeth to the Ephesians on this wise: 'By
grace are ye saved through faith, and that not of yourselves,
for it is the gift of God, and not of works, lest any man
should glory.'[11] And, to be short, the sum of all Paul's
disputation is this, that if justice come of works then it cometh not of grace, and if it come of grace then it cometh not
of works. And to this end tend all the prophets, as St. Peter
saith in the tenth of the Acts: 'Of Christ all the prophets,'
saith St. Peter, 'do witness that through his name all they
that believe in him shall receive remission of sins.'[12]

And after this wise to be justified only by this true and
lively faith in Christ speak all the old and ancient authors,
both Greeks and Latins, of whom I will specially rehearse
three, Hilary, Basil and Ambrose. St. Hilary saith these
words plainly in the ninth canon upon Matthew: 'Faith only

justifieth.' And St. Basil, a Greek author, writeth thus: 'This is a perfect and whole rejoicing in God, when a man advanceth not himself for his own righteousness, but acknowledgeth himself to lack true justice and righteousness and to be justified by the only faith in Christ. And Paul,' saith he, 'doth glory in the contempt of his own righteousness, and that he looketh for the righteousness of God by faith.'[13] These be the very words of St. Basil; and St. Ambrose, a Latin author, saith these words: 'This is the ordinance of God, that they who believe in Christ should be saved without works, by faith only, freely receiving remission of their sins.'

Consider diligently these words, 'without works, by faith only, we receive remission of our sins.' What can be spoken more plainly than to say that freely without works, by faith only, we obtain remission of our sins? These and other like sentences that we be justified by faith only, freely, and without works, we do read ofttimes in the most and best writers; as, beside Hilary, Basil and St. Ambrose, before rehearsed, we read the same in Origen, St. Chrysostom, St. Cyprian, St. Augustine, Prosper, Ecumenius, Photius, Bernard, Anselm, and many other authors, Greek and Latin.

Nevertheless, this sentence, that we be justified by faith only, is not so meant of them that the said justifying faith is alone in man, without true repentance, hope, charity, dread, and the fear of God, at any time and season. Nor when they say that we be justified freely they mean not that we should or might afterward be idle, and that nothing should be required on our parts afterward; neither they mean not so to be justified without good works that we should do no good works at all, like as shall be more expressed at large hereafter. But this saying, that we be justified by faith only, freely, and without works, is spoken for to take away clearly all merit of our works, as being unable to deserve our justification at God's hands, and thereby most plainly to express the weakness of man and the goodness of God, the great infirmity of ourselves and the might and power of God, the imperfectness of our own works and the most abundant grace of our Saviour Christ, and therefore wholly to ascribe the merit and deserving of our justification unto Christ only and his most precious bloodshedding.

This faith the Holy Scripture teacheth us. This is the

strong rock and foundation of Christian religion. This doctrine all old and ancient authors of Christ's Church do approve. This doctrine advanceth and setteth forth the true
glory of Christ and beateth down vainglory of man. This
whosoever denieth is not to be accounted for a Christian
man nor for a setter forth of Christ's glory, but for an adversary of Christ and his Gospel and for a setter forth of man's
vainglory. And although this doctrine be never so true (as it
is most true indeed), that we be justified freely, without all
merit of our own good works (as St. Paul doth express it),[14]
and freely by this lively and perfect faith in Christ only (as the
ancient authors used to speak it), yet this true doctrine
must be also truly understood and most plainly declared,
lest carnal men should take unjustly occasion thereby to
live carnally, after the appetite and will of the world, the
flesh, and the devil. And because no man should err by mis-
taking of this doctrine, I shall plainly and shortly so declare
the right understanding of the same that no man shall justly think that he may thereby take any occasion of carnal
liberty, to follow the desires of the flesh, or that thereby any
kind of sin shall be committed or any ungodly living the
more used.

First, you shall understand that in our justification by
Christ it is not all one thing, the office of God unto man and
the office of man unto God. Justification is not the office of
man, but of God; for man cannot make himself righteous by
his own works, neither in part nor in the whole; for that were
the greatest arrogancy and presumption of man that Antichrist could set up against God, to affirm that a man
might by his own works take away and purge his own sins,
and so justify himself. But justification is the office of God
only, and is not a thing which we render unto him, but which
we receive of him; not which we give to him, but which we
take of him, by his free mercy and by the only merits of his
most dearly beloved Son, our only redeemer, saviour, and
justifier, Jesus Christ: so that the true understanding of
this doctrine, we be justified freely by faith without works,
or that we be justified by faith in Christ only, is not that this
our own act to believe in Christ, or this our faith in Christ
which is within us, doth justify us and deserve our justification unto us (for that were to count ourselves to be justified
by some act or virtue that is within ourselves); but the true

understanding and meaning thereof is that, although we hear God's word and believe it, although we have faith, hope, charity, repentance, dread and fear of God within us, and do never so many good works thereunto, yet we must renounce the merit of all our said virtues, of faith, hope, charity, and all other virtues and good deeds which we either have done, shall do, or can do, as things that be far too weak and insufficient and imperfect to deserve remission of our sins and our justification; and therefore we must trust only in God's mercy and that sacrifice which our high priest and saviour Christ Jesus, the Son of God, once offered for us upon the cross, to obtain thereby God's grace and remission, as well of our original sin in baptism as of all actual sin committed by us after our baptism, if we truly repent and turn unfeignedly to him again. So that, as St. John Baptist, although he were never so virtuous and godly a man, yet in this matter of forgiving of sin he did put the people from him and pointed them unto Christ, saying thus unto them: 'Behold, yonder is the lamb of God who taketh away the sins of the world,'[15] even so, as great and as godly a virtue as the lively faith is, yet it putteth us from itself and remitteth or pointeth us unto Christ, for to have only by him remission of our sins, or justification. So that our faith in Christ (as it were) saith unto us thus: 'It is not I that take away your sins, but it is Christ only, and to him only I send you for that purpose, forsaking therein all your good virtues, words, thoughts, and works, and only putting your trust in Christ.'

The Third Part of the Sermon of Salvation

It hath been manifestly declared unto you that no man can fufill the law of God, and therefore by the law all men are condemned; whereupon it followeth necessarily that some other thing should be required for our salvation than the law: and that is a true and lively faith in Christ, bringing forth good works and a life according to God's commandments. And also you heard the ancient authors' minds of this saying, 'faith in Christ only justifieth man,' so plainly declared that you see that the very true meaning of this proposition or saying, 'we be justified by faith in Christ only,' (according to the meaning of the old ancient authors)

is this: We put our faith in Christ, that we be justified by him
only, that we be justified by God's free mercy and the merits
of our Saviour Christ only, and by no virtue or good work of
our own that is in us, or that we can be able to have or to do
for to deserve the same, Christ himself only being the cause
meritorious thereof.

Here you perceive many words to be used to avoid contention in words with them that delight to brawl about words,
and also to show the true meaning to avoid evil taking and
misunderstanding; and yet peradventure all will not serve
with them that be contentious, but contenders will ever
forge matters of contention, even when they have none occasion thereto. Notwithstanding, such be the less to be
passed upon, so that the rest may profit who will be more
desirous to know the truth than (when it is plain enough) to
contend about it, and with contentious and captious cavil-
lation to obscure and darken it. Truth it is that our own
works do not justify us, to speak properly of our justification; that is to say, our works do not merit or deserve
remission of our sins and make us, of unjust, just before
God; but God of his own mercy, through the only merits and
deservings of his Son Jesus Christ, doth justify us. Nevertheless, because faith doth directly send us to Christ for
remission of our sins, and that by faith given us of God, we
embrace the promise of God's mercy and of the remission of
our sins (which thing none other of our virtues or works
properly doth) therefore Scripture useth to say that faith
without works doth justify.

And forasmuch that it is all one sentence in effect to say
faith without works and only faith doth justify us, therefore
the old ancient fathers of the Church from time to time have
uttered our justification with this speech, 'Only faith
justifieth us,' meaning none other thing than St. Paul meant
when he said, 'Faith without works justifieth us.'[16] And
because all this is brought to pass through the only merits
and deservings of our Saviour Christ, and not through our
merits or through the merit of any virtue that we have
within us or of any work that cometh from us, therefore, in
that respect of merit and deserving, we forsake, as it were,
altogether again faith, works and all other virtues. For our
own imperfection is so great, through the corruption of
original sin, that all is imperfect that is within us, faith,

charity, hope, dread, thoughts, words and works, and therefore not apt to merit and deserve any part of our justification for us. And this form of speaking we use in the humbling of ourselves to God and to give all the glory to our Saviour Christ, who is best worthy to have it.

Here you have heard the office of God in our justification, and how we receive it of him freely, by his mercy, without our deserts, through true and lively faith. Now you shall hear the office and duty of a Christian man unto God, what we ought on our part to render unto God again for his great mercy and goodness. Our office is not to pass the time of this present life unfruitfully and idly after that we are baptized or justified, not caring how few good works we do to the glory of God and profit of our neighbours; much less is it our office after that we be once made Christ's members to live contrary to the same, making ourselves members of the devil, walking after his enticements and after the suggestions of the world and the flesh, whereby we know that we do serve the world and the devil and not God.

For that faith which bringeth forth (without repentance) either evil works or no good works is not a right, pure, and lively faith, but a dead, devilish, counterfeit, and feigned faith, as St. Paul and St. James call it.[17] For even the devils know and believe that Christ was born of a virgin, that he fasted forty days and forty nights without meat and drink, that he wrought all kinds of miracles, declaring himself very God; they believe also that Christ for our sakes suffered most painful death to redeem us from everlasting death, and that he rose again from death the third day; they believe that he ascended into heaven and that he sitteth on the right hand of the Father, and at the last end of this world shall come again and judge both the quick and the dead. These articles of our faith the devils believe, and so they believe all things that be written in the New and Old Testament to be true; and yet for all this faith they be but devils, remaining still in their damnable estate, lacking the very true Christian faith.[18] For the right and true Christian faith is not only to believe that Holy Scripture and all the foresaid articles of our faith are true, but also to have a sure trust and confidence in God's merciful promises, to be saved from everlasting damnation by Christ, whereof doth follow a loving heart to obey his commandments.

And this true Christian faith neither any devil hath nor yet
any man who, in the outward profession of his mouth and in
his outward receiving of the sacraments, in coming to the
church, and in all other outward appearances seemeth to be
a Christian man, and yet in his living and deeds showeth the
contrary. For how can a man have this true faith, this sure
trust and confidence in God that by the merits of Christ his
sins be forgiven, and he reconciled to the favour of God, and
to be partaker of the kingdom of heaven by Christ, when he
liveth ungodly and denieth Christ in his deeds? Surely no
such ungodly man can have this faith and trust in God. For
as they know Christ to be the only saviour of the world, so
they know also that wicked men shall not enjoy the kingdom of God. They know that God hateth unrighteousness,
that he will destroy all those that speak untruly, that those
who have done good works (which cannot be done without
a lively faith in Christ) shall come forth into the resurrection
of life, and those that have done evil shall come unto the
resurrection of judgment. Very well they know also that to
them that be contentious, and to them that will not be obe-
dient unto the truth but will obey unrighteousness, shall
come indignation, wrath and affliction, etc.

Therefore, to conclude, considering the infinite benefits
of God showed and given unto us mercifully without our
deserts, who hath not only created us of nothing and from
a piece of vile clay of his infinite goodness hath exalted us,
as touching our soul, unto his own similitude and likeness,
but also, whereas we were condemned to hell and death
everlasting, hath given his own natural Son, being God eternal, immortal, and equal unto himself in power and glory, to
be incarnated, and to take our mortal nature upon him,
with the infirmities of the same, and in the same nature to
suffer most shameful and painful death for our offences, to
the intent to justify us and to restore us to life everlasting,
so making us also his dear children, brethren unto his only
Son our Saviour Christ, and inheritors for ever with him of
his everlasting kingdom of heaven.

These great and merciful benefits of God, if they be well
considered, do neither minister unto us occasion to be idle
and to live without doing any good works, neither yet stir us
up by any means to do evil things; but contrariwise, if we be
not desperate persons and our hearts harder than stones,

they move us to render ourselves unto God wholly, with all our will, hearts, might and power, to serve him in all good deeds, obeying his commandments during our lives, to seek in all things his glory and honour, not our sensual pleasures and vainglory, evermore dreading willingly to offend such a merciful God and loving Redeemer in word, thought, or deed. And the said benefits of God, deeply considered, move us for his sake also to be ever ready to give ourselves to our neighbours and, as much as lieth in us, to study with all our endeavour to do good to every man. These be the fruits of true faith, to do good as much as lieth in us to every man and, above all things, to advance the glory of God, of whom only we have our sanctification, justification, salvation and redemption: to whom be glory, praise and honour, world without end. Amen.

III

Richard Hooker

A Learned Discourse of Justification,
Works, and how the Foundation
of Faith is Overthrown

> 'The wicked doth compass about the righteous;
> therefore perverse judgment doth proceed.'
>
> Habakkuk 1:4

For better manifestation of the prophet's meaning in this place we are, first, to consider 'the wicked,' of whom he saith that they 'compass about the righteous'; secondly, 'the righteous' that are compassed about by them; and, thirdly, that which is inferred, 'therefore perverse judgment proceedeth.' Touching the first, there are two kinds of wicked men, of whom in the fifth of the former to the Corinthians the blessed Apostle speaketh thus: 'Do ye not judge them that are within? But God judgeth them that are without.'[1] There are wicked, therefore, whom the Church may judge, and there are wicked whom God only judgeth; wicked within and wicked without the walls of the Church. If within the Church particular persons, being apparently such, cannot otherwise be reformed, the rule of apostolical judgment is this: 'Separate them from among them you';[2] if whole assemblies, this: 'Separate yourselves from among them; for what society hath light with darkness?'[3] But the wicked whom the prophet meaneth were Babylonians, and therefore without. For which cause we have heard at large heretofore in what sort he urgeth God to judge them.

Now concerning the righteous, there neither is nor ever

61

was any mere natural man absolutely righteous in himself:
that is to say, void of all unrighteousness, of all sin. We dare
not except, no not the blessed Virgin herself, of whom although we say with St. Augustine, for the honour's sake
which we owe to our Lord and Saviour Christ, we are not willing, in this cause, to move any question of his mother; yet
forasmuch as the schools of Rome have made it a question,
we must answer with Eusebius Emissenus,[4] who speaketh of
her, and to her, to this effect: 'Thou didst by special prerog-
ative nine months together entertain within the closet of
thy flesh the hope of all the ends of the earth, the honour of
the world, the common joy of men. He, from whom all things
had their beginning, hath had his own beginning from thee;
of thy body he took the blood which was to be shed for the
life of the world; of thee he took that which even for thee he
paid. The mother of the Redeemer herself, otherwise than
by redemption, is not loosed from the band of that ancient
sin.' If Christ have paid a ransom for all,[5] even for her it
followeth that all without exception were captives. If one
have died for all, all were dead, dead in sin;[6] all sinful,
therefore none absolutely righteous in themselves; but we
are absolutely righteous in Christ. The world then must
show a Christian man, otherwise it is not able to show a man
that is perfectly righteous: 'Christ is made unto us wisdom,
justice,[7] sanctification, and redemption':[8] wisdom, because
he hath revealed his Father's will; justice, because he hath
offered himself a sacrifice for sin; sanctification, because
he hath given us of his Spirit; redemption, because he hath
appointed a day to vindicate his children out of the bands of
corruption into liberty which is glorious.[9] How Christ is
made wisdom, and how redemption, it may be declared
when occasion serveth; but how Christ is made the
righteousness of men we are now to declare.

There is a glorifying righteousness of men in the world to
come; and there is a justifying and a sanctifying righteousness here. The righteousness wherewith we shall be clothed
in the world to come is both perfect and inherent. That whereby we are justified is perfect, but not inherent. That whereby
we are sanctified, inherent, but not perfect. This openeth a
way to the plain understanding of that grand question, which
hangeth yet in controversy between us and the Church of
Rome, about the matter of justifying righteousness.

First, although they imagine that the mother of our Lord and Saviour Jesus Christ were, for his honour, and by his special protection, preserved clean from all sin, yet touching the rest they teach, as we do, that all have sinned; that infants who did never actually offend have their natures defiled, destitute of justice, and averted from God.[10] They teach, as we do, that God doth justify the soul of man alone, without any other coefficient cause of justice; that, in making man righteous none do work efficiently with God, but God.[11] They teach, as we do, that unto justice no man ever attained, but by the merits of Jesus Christ.[12] They teach, as we do, that although Christ as God be the efficient, as man the meritorious, cause of our justice, yet in us also there is something required.[13] God is the cause of our natural life; in him we live: but he quickeneth not the body without the soul in the body. Christ hath merited to make us just; but as a medicine which is made for health doth not heal by being made but by being applied, so by the merits of Christ there can be no justification without the application of his merits. Thus far we join hands with the Church of Rome.

Doctrinal disagreement

Wherein then do we disagree? We disagree about the nature of the very essence of the medicine whereby Christ cureth our disease; about the manner of applying it; about the number and the power of means, which God requireth in us for the effectual applying thereof to our soul's comfort.

When they are required to show what the righteousness is whereby a Christian man is justified, they answer that it is a divine spiritual quality, which quality, received into the soul, doth first make it to be one of them who are born of God; and, secondly, endue it with power to bring forth such works as they do that are born of him; even as the soul of man, being joined unto his body, doth first make him to be in the number of reasonable creatures, and, secondly, enable him to perform the natural functions which are proper to his kind; that it maketh the soul gracious and amiable in the sight of God, in regard whereof it is termed grace; that by it, through the merit of Christ, we are delivered as from sin, so from eternal death and condemnation, the reward of sin. This grace they will have to be applied by infusion, to the end that, as the body is warm by the heat which is in the body, so the soul might be righteous by inherent grace; which grace they make capable of increase; as the body may be more and more warm, so the soul more and more justified, according as grace shall be augmented; the augmentation whereof is merited by good works, as good works are made meritorious by it.[14] Wherefore the first receipt of grace is in their divinity the first justification; the second thereof, the second justification.

As grace may be increased by the merit of good works, so it may be diminished by the demerit of sins venial; it may be lost by mortal sin.[15] Inasmuch, therefore, as it is needful in the one case to repair, in the other to recover, the loss which is made, the infusion of grace hath her sundry after-meals; for which cause they make many ways to apply the infusion of grace. It is applied unto infants through baptism, without either faith or works, and in them it really taketh away original sin and the punishment due unto it; it is applied unto infidels and wicked men in their first justification through baptism, without works, yet not without faith; and it taketh away both sin actual and original, together with all whatsoever punishment eternal or temporal thereby deserved. Unto such as have attained the first justification, that is to say, the first receipt of grace, it is applied further by good works to the increase of former grace, which is the second justification. If they work more and more, grace doth more and more increase, and they are more and more justified.

To such as have diminished it by venial sins it is applied by holy water, Ave Marias, crossings, papal salutations, and such like, which serve for reparations of grace decayed. To such as have lost it through mortal sin, it is applied by the sacrament (as they term it) of penance; which sacrament hath force to confer grace anew, yet in such sort that, being so conferred, it hath not altogether so much power as at the first. For it only cleanseth out the stain or guilt of sin committed, and changeth the punishment eternal into a temporary satisfactory punishment here, if time do serve, if not, hereafter to be endured, except it be either lightened by masses, works of charity, pilgrimages, fasts, and such like; or else shortened by pardon for term, or by plenary pardon quite removed and taken away.[16]

This is the mystery of the man of sin. This maze the Church of Rome doth cause her followers to tread when they ask her the way of justification. I cannot stand now to unrip this building and to sift it piece by piece; only I will set up a frame of apostolical erection by it in a few words, that it may befall Babylon, in presence of that which God hath builded, as it happened unto Dagon before the ark.

'Doubtless,' saith the Apostle, 'I have counted all things but loss, and I do judge them to be dung, that I may win Christ, and be found in him, not having mine own righteousness, but that which is through the faith of Christ, the righteousness which is of God through faith.'[17] Whether they speak of the first or second justification, they make the essence of it a divine quality inherent, they make it righteousness which is in us. If it be in us, then it is ours, as our souls are ours, though we have them from God and can hold them no longer than pleaseth him; for if he withdraw the breath of our nostrils we fall to dust; but the righteousness wherein we must be found, if we will be justified, is not our own: therefore we cannot be justified by any inherent quality. Christ hath merited righteousness for as many as are found in him. In him God findeth us, if we be faithful, for by faith we are incorporated into him.

Then, although in ourselves we be altogether sinful and unrighteous, yet even the man who in himself is impious, full of iniquity, full of sin, him being found in Christ through faith, and having his sin in hatred through repentance, him God beholdeth with a gracious eye, putteth away his sin by not imputing it, taketh quite away the punishment due thereunto, by pardoning it, and accepteth him in Jesus Christ as perfectly righteous, as if he had fulfilled all that is commanded him in the law: shall I say more perfectly righteous than if himself had fulfilled the whole law? I must take heed what I say; but the Apostle saith, 'God made him who knew no sin to be sin for us, that we might be made the righteousness of God in him.'[18] Such we are in the sight of God the Father as is the very Son of God himself. Let it be counted folly, or phrensy, or fury, or whatsoever. It is our wisdom and our comfort; we care for no knowledge in the world but this, that man hath sinned and God hath suffered; that God hath made himself the sin of men, and that men are made the righteousness of God.

You see therefore that the Church of Rome, in teaching justification by inherent grace, doth pervert the truth of Christ, and that by the hands of his Apostles we have received otherwise than she teacheth.

Sanctification

Now concerning the righteousness of sanctification, we deny it not to be inherent; we grant that, unless we work, we have it not; only we distinguish it as a thing in nature different from the righteousness of justification: we are righteous the one way by the faith of Abraham, the other way, except we do the works of Abraham, we are not righteous. Of the one, St. Paul, 'To him that worketh not, but believeth, faith is counted for righteousness.'[19] Of the other, St. John, 'He is righteous who worketh righteousness.'[20] Of the one, St. Paul doth prove by Abraham's example that we have it of faith without works.[21] Of the other, St. James by Abraham's example, that by works we have it, and not only by faith.[22] St. Paul doth plainly sever these two parts of Christian righteousness one from the other; for in the sixth to the Romans he writeth, 'Being freed from sin and made servants of God, ye have your fruit in holiness, and the end everlasting life.'[23] 'Ye are made free from sin and made servants unto God'; this is the righteousness of justification; 'Ye have your fruit in holiness': this is the righteousness of sanctification. By the one we are interested in the right of inheriting; by the other we are brought to the actual possessing of eternal bliss, and so the end is everlasting life.

The prophet Habakkuk doth here[24] term the Jews' 'righteous men,' not only because being justified by faith they were free from sin, but also because they had their measure of fruit in holiness. According to whose example of charitable judgment, which leaveth it to God to discern what men are, and speaketh of them according to that which they do profess themselves to be, although they be not holy whom men do think, but whom God doth know indeed to be such; yet let every Christian man know that in Christian equity he standeth bound so to think and speak of his brethren as of men that have a measure in the fruit of holiness and a right unto the titles wherewith God, in token of special favour and mercy, vouchsafeth to honour his chosen servants. So we see the Apostles of our Saviour Christ do use everywhere the name of *saints;* so the prophet the name of *righteous.* But let us all endeavour to be such as we desire to be termed: 'Godly names do not justify godless men,' saith Salvianus. We are but upbraided when we are honoured with names and titles whereunto our lives and manners are not suitable.

If we have indeed our fruit in holiness, notwithstanding we must note that the more we abound therein the more need we have to crave that we may be strengthened and supported. Our very virtues may be snares unto us. The enemy that waiteth for all occasions to work our ruin hath ever found it harder to overthrow a humble sinner than a proud saint. There is no man's case so dangerous as his, whom Satan hath persuaded that his own righteousness shall present him pure and blameless in the sight of God. If we could say, 'we are not guilty of anything at all in our own consciences' (we know ourselves far from this innocency, we cannot say we know nothing by ourselves, but if we could) should we therefore plead not guilty in the presence of our Judge that sees further into our hearts than we ourselves are able to see? If our hands did never offer violence to our brethren, a bloody thought doth prove us murderers before him.[25] If we had never opened our mouths to utter any scandalous, offensive, or hurtful word, the cry of our secret cogitations is head in the ears of God. If we did not commit the evils which we do daily and hourly, either in deeds, words, or thoughts, yet in the good things which we do how many defects are there intermingled!

God, in that which is done, respecteth specially the mind and intention of the doer. Cut off then all those things wherein we have regarded our own glory, those things which we do to please men or to satisfy our own liking, those things which we do with any by-respect,[26] not sincerely and purely for the love of God, and a small score will serve for the number of our righteous deeds. Let the holiest and best thing that we do be considered: we are never better affected unto God than when we pray; yet when we pray how are our affections many times distracted! How little reverence do we show to the grand majesty of that God unto whom we speak! How little remorse of our own miseries! How little taste of the sweet influence of his tender mercy do we feel!

Are we not as unwilling many times to begin, and as glad to make an end, as if God in saying 'Call upon me' had set us a very burdensome task?

It may seem somewhat extreme which I shall speak; therefore let every man judge of it even as his own heart shall tell him, and no otherwise. I will but only make a demand: if God should yield to us, not as unto Abraham, if fifty, forty, thirty, twenty, yea, or if ten good persons could be found in a city, for their sakes that city should not be destroyed; [27] but if God should make us an offer thus large: 'Search all the generations of men since the fall of your father Adam, find one man that hath done any one action which hath passed from him pure, without any stain or blemish at all, and for that one man's one only action neither man nor angel shall feel the torments which are prepared for both'—do you think that this ransom, to deliver men and angels, would be found among the sons of men? The best things we do have somewhat in them to be pardoned. How then can we do anything meritorious and worthy to be rewarded.?

Indeed, God doth liberally promise whatsoever appertaineth to a blessed life unto as many as sincerely keep his law, though they be not able exactly to keep it. Wherefore we acknowledge a dutiful necessity of doing well, but the meritorious dignity of well doing we utterly renounce. We see how far we are from the perfect righteousness of the law. The little fruit which we have in holiness, it is, God knoweth, corrupt and unsound: we put no confidence at all in it, we challenge nothing in the world for it, we dare not call God to a reckoning, as if we had him in our debt-books. Our continual suit to him is, and must be, to bear with our infirmities, to pardon our offences.

But the people of whom the prophet speaketh, were they all, or were the most part of them, such as had care to walk uprightly? Did they thirst after righteousness? Did they wish, did they long with the righteous prophet, 'O that our ways were made so direct that we might keep thy statutes'?[28] Did they lament with the righteous apostle, 'Miserable men, the good which we wish and purpose, and strive to do, we cannot'?[29] No, the words of other prophets concerning this people do show the contrary. How grievously doth Isaiah mourn over them: 'Ah sinful nation, people laden with ini-

quity, wicked seed, corrupt children'![30] All which notwithstanding, so wide are the bowels of his compassion enlarged
that he denieth us not, no not when we are laden with iniquity,
leave to commune familiarly with him, liberty to crave and
entreat that what plagues soever we have deserved we may
not be in worse case than unbelievers, that we may not be
hemmed in by pagans and infidels. Jerusalem is a sinful
polluted city; but Jerusalem compared with Babylon is righteous. And shall the righteous be overborne, shall they be
compassed about by the wicked? But the prophet doth not
only complain, 'Lord, how cometh it to pass that thou
handlest us so hardly over whom thy name is called, and
bearest with heathen nations that despise thee?' No, he
breaketh out through extremity of grief and inferreth thus
violently: This proceeding is perverse; the righteous are
thus handled, 'therefore perverse judgment doth proceed.'[31]

The salvation of 'our fathers'

Which illation[32] containeth many things whereof it were
much better both for you to hear and me to speak, if
necessity did not draw me to another task. Paul and Barnabas being requested to preach the same things again
which once they had preached,[33] thought it their duties to
satisfy the godly desires of men sincerely affected towards
the truth. Nor may it seem burdensome to me, or for you unprofitable, that I follow their example, the like occasion unto theirs being offered me. When we had last the Epistle of
St. Paul to the Hebrews[34] in our hands, and of that epistle
these words, 'In these last days he hath spoken unto us by
his Son';[35] after we had thence collected the nature of the
visible Church of Christ, and had defined it to be a community of men sanctified through the profession of that
truth which God hath taught the world by his Son; and had
declared that the scope of Christian doctrine is the comfort
of them whose hearts are overcharged with the burden of
sin; and had proved that the doctrine professed in the
Church of Rome doth bereave men of comfort, both in their
lives and at their deaths; the conclusion in the end whereunto we came was this: 'The Church of Rome being in faith
so corrupted as she is, and refusing to be reformed as she
doth, we are to sever ourselves from her. The example of our

fathers may not retain us in communion and fellowship with
that church, under hope that we, so continuing, might be
saved as well as they. God, I doubt not, was merciful to save
thousands of them, though they lived in popish superstitions, inasmuch as they sinned ignorantly; but the truth is
now laid open before our eyes.' The former part of this last
sentence, namely, these words. 'I doubt not but *God was
merciful to save thousands of our fathers living in popish
superstitions, inasmuch as they sinned ignorantly'* — this
sentence I beseech you to mark, and to sift it with the strict
severity of austere judgment, that if it be found as gold it
may stand, suitable to the precious foundation whereupon
it was then laid; for I protest that if it be hay or stubble mine
own hand shall set fire to it.[36] Two questions have risen by
occasion of the speech before alleged: the one, whether our
fathers, infected with popish errors and superstitions,
might be saved; the other, whether their ignorance be a
reasonable inducement to make us think that they might.
We are therefore to examine first what possibility, and then
what probability, there is that God might be merciful unto
so many of our fathers.

So many of our fathers living in popish superstitions, yet
by the mercy of God to be saved? No, this could not be: God
hath spoken by his angel from heaven unto his people concerning Babylon (by Babylon we understand the Church of
Rome), 'Go out of her, my people, that ye be not partakers of
her sins, and that ye receive not of her plagues.'[37] For
answer whereunto, first, I do not take these words to be
meant only of temporal plagues, of the corporal death, sorrow, famine, and fire whereunto God in his wrath hath condemned Babylon; and that to save his chosen people from
these plagues he saith, 'Go out'; and with like intent, as in
the Gospel, speaking of Jerusalem's desolation he saith,
'Let them that are in Judea flee unto the mountains, and
them who are in the midst thereof depart out';[38] or as in
former times unto Lot, 'Arise, take thy wife and thy
daughters who are here, lest thou be destroyed in the
punishment of the city';[39] but forasmuch as here it is said,
'Go out of Babylon that ye be not partakers of her sins, and
by consequence of her plagues,' plagues eternal being due
to the sins of Babylon, no doubt their everlasting destruc-
tion, who are partakers herein, is either principally meant

or necessarily implied in this sentence. How then was it possible for so many of our fathers to be saved, since they were
so far from departing out of Babylon that they took her for
their mother and in her bosom yielded up the ghost?

First, the plagues being threatened unto them that are
partakers in the sins of Babylon; we can define nothing concerning our fathers out of this sentence, unless we show
what the sins of Babylon be, and who they be that are such
partakers in them that their everlasting plagues are inevitable. The sins which may be common both to them of the
Church of Rome and to others departed thence must be
severed from this question. He who saith, 'Depart out of
Babylon lest ye be partakers of her sins', showeth plainly
that he meaneth such sins as, except we separate ourselves, we have no power in the world to avoid; such im-
pieties as by law they have established, and whereunto all
that are among them either do indeed assent or else are by
powerable means forced in show and in appearance to subject themselves: as, for example, in the Church of Rome it is
maintained that the same credit and reverence which we
give to the Scriptures of God ought also to be given to
unwritten verities; that the pope is supreme head ministe-
rial over the universal Church militant; that the bread in the
eucharist is transubstantiated into Christ; that it is to be
adored, and to be offered up unto God as a sacrifice propi-
tiatory for quick and dead; that images are to be worshipped, saints to be called upon as intercessors, and such like.

Now, because some heresies do concern things only
believed; as transubstantiating of sacramental elements in
the eucharist; some concern things which are practised
also and put in ure,[40] as adoration of the elements transubstantiated, we must note that the practice of that is
sometimes received whereof the doctrine which teacheth it
is not heretically maintained. They are all partakers in the
maintenance of heresies who by word or deed allow them,
knowing them, although not knowing them to be heresies;
as also they, and that most dangerously of all others, who,
knowing heresy to be heresy, do notwithstanding, in worldly
respects, make semblance of allowing that which in heart
and in judgment they condemn. But heresy is heretically
maintained by such as obstinately hold it after wholesome
admonition. Of the last sort, as also of the next before, I

make no doubt but that their condemnation, without actual repentance, is inevitable. Lest any man therefore should think that in speaking of our fathers I speak indifferently of them all, let my words, I beseech you, be well noted: 'I doubt not but God was merciful to save thousands of our fathers'; which thing I will now by God's assistance set more plainly before your eyes.

Many are partakers of the error who are not of the heresy of the Church of Rome. The people, following the conduct of their guides, and observing as they did exactly that which was prescribed them, thought they did God good service, when indeed they did dishonor him. This was their error. But the heresies of the Church of Rome, their dogmatical positions opposite unto Christian truth, what one man among ten thousand did ever understand? Of them who understand Roman heresies, and allow them, all are not alike partakers in the action of allowing. Some allow them as the first founders and establishers of them, which crime toucheth none but their popes and councils. The people are clear and free from this. Of them who maintain popish heresy not as authors, but receivers of it from others, all maintain it not as masters. In this are not the people partakers neither, but only their predicants and their schoolmen.[41] Of them who have been partakers in the sin of teaching popish heresy there is also a difference; for they have not all been teachers of all popish heresies. 'Put a difference,' saith St. Jude; 'have compassion upon some.'[42] Shall we lap up all in one condition? Shall we cast them all headlong? Shall we plunge them all in that infernal and ever-flaming lake — them who have been partakers in the error of Babylon together with them within the heresy — them who have been the authors of heresy with them that by terror and violence have been forced to receive it — them who have taught it with them whose simplicity hath by sleights and conveyances of false teachers been seduced to believe it — them who have been partakers in one with them who have been partakers in many — them who in many with them who in all?

Notwithstanding I grant that, although the condemnation of one be more tolerable than of another, yet from the man that laboureth at the plough to him that sitteth in the Vatican, to all partakers in the sins of Babylon, our fathers, though they did but erroneously practise that which their guides did heretically teach, to all without exception plagues worldly were due. The pit is ordinarily the end as well of the guided as the guide in blindness. But woe worth the hour wherein we were born, except we might persuade ourselves better things, things that accompany men's salvation,[43] even where we know that worse and such as accompany condemnation are due. Then must we show some way how possibly they might escape.

The way to escape judgment

What way is there for sinners to escape the judgment of God but only by appealing unto the seat of his saving mercy? Which mercy we do not with Origen extend unto devils and damned spirits. God hath mercy upon thousands, but there be thousands also who be hardened. Christ hath therefore set the bounds; he hath fixed the limits of his saving mercy within the compass of these two terms. In the third of St. John's Gospel, mercy is restrained to believers. 'God sent not his Son to condemn the world, but that the world through his might be saved. He that believeth shall not be condemned; he that believeth not is condemned already, because he believeth not in the Son of God.'[44] In the second of the Revelation, mercy is restrained to the penitent; for of Jezebel and her sectaries thus he speaketh: 'I gave her space to repent and she repented not. Behold, I will cast her into a bed, and them that commit fornication with her into great affliction, except they repent them of their works; and I will kill her children with death.'[45] Our hope therefore of the fathers is vain if they were altogether faithless and impenitent.

They be not all faithless that are either weak in assenting to the truth or stiff in maintaining things any way opposite to the truth of Christian doctrine. But as many as hold the foundation which is precious, although they hold it but weakly and as it were by a slender thread, although they frame many base and unsuitable things upon it, things that cannot abide the trial of the fire, yet shall they pass the fiery trial and be saved, who indeed have builded themselves upon the rock which is the foundation of the Church.[46] If then our fathers did not hold the foundation of faith, there is no doubt but they were faithless. If many of them held it, then is there herein no impediment but that many of them might be saved. Then let us see what the foundation of faith is, and whether we may think that thousands of our fathers living in popish superstitions did notwithstanding hold the foundation.

If the foundation of faith do import the general ground whereupon we rest when we do believe, the writings of the Evangelists and Apostles are the foundation of Christian faith: 'We believe it because we read it,' saith St. Jerome.[47] O that the Church of Rome did as soundly interpret those fundamental writings whereupon we build our faith as she doth willingly hold and embrace them!

But if the name *foundation* do note the principal thing which is believed, then is that the foundation of our faith which St. Paul hath unto Timothy: 'God manifested in the flesh, justified in the spirit, etc.';[48] that of Nathanael: 'Thou art the Son of the living God, thou art the king of Israel';[49] that of the inhabitants of Samaria: 'This is Christ, the Saviour of the world.'[50] He that directly denieth this doth utterly raze the very foundation of our faith. I have proved heretofore that, although the Church of Rome hath played the harlot worse than ever did Israel, yet are they not, as now the synagogue of the Jews which plainly denieth Christ Jesus,[51] quite and clean excluded from the new covenant. But as Samaria compared with Jerusalem is termed *Aholah*, a church or tabernacle of her own, contrariwise Jerusalem *Aholibah*, the resting place of the Lord;[52] so whatsoever we term the Church of Rome when we compare her to reformed churches, still we put a difference, as then between Babylon and Samaria, so now between Rome and heathenish assemblies. Which opinion I must and will recall; I must grant, and will, that the Church of Rome together with all her children is clean excluded: there is no difference in the world between our fathers and Saracens, Turks, or Painims, if they did directly deny Christ crucified for the salvation of the world.

But how many millions of them are known so to have ended their mortal lives that the drawing of their breath hath ceased with the uttering of this faith: 'Christ my Saviour, my Redeemer Jesus!' And shall we say that such did not hold the foundation of Christian faith? Answer is made that this they might unfeignedly confess, and yet be far enough from salvation. For behold, saith the Apostle, 'I, Paul, say unto you that if ye be circumcised Christ shall profit you nothing.'[53] Christ, in the work of man's salvation, is alone: the Galatians were cast away by joining circumcision and other rites of the law with Christ. The Church of Rome doth teach her children to join other things likewise with him; therefore their faith, their belief, doth not profit them anything at all.

It is true, they do indeed join other things with Christ; but how? Not in the work of redemption itself, which they grant that Christ alone hath performed sufficiently for the salvation of the whole world; but in the application of this inestimable treasure, that it may be effectual to their salvation, how demurely soever they confess that they seek remission of sins no otherwise than by the blood of Christ, using humbly the means appointed by him to apply the benefit of his holy blood, they teach, indeed, so many things pernicious to the Christian faith, in setting down the means whereof they speak, that the very foundation of faith which they hold is thereby plainly overthrown, and the force of the blood of Jesus Christ extinguished. We may therefore dispute with them, press them, urge them even with as dangerous sequels as the Apostle doth the Galatians.

But I demand, if some of those Galatians, heartily embracing the Gospel of Christ, sincere and sound in faith, this only error excepted, had ended their lives before they were ever taught how perilous an opinion they held, shall we think that the damage of this error did so overweigh the benefit of their faith that the mercy of God, his mercy, might not save them? I grant that they overthrew the very foundation of faith by consequent. Doth not that so likewise which the Lutheran churches do at this day so stiffly and so fiercely maintain?[54] For mine own part, I dare not hereupon deny the possibility of their salvation who have been the chiefest instruments of ours, albeit they carried to their grave a persuasion so greatly repugnant to the truth. Forasmuch therefore as it may be said of the Church of Rome, 'She hath yet a little strength,'[55] she doth not directly deny the foundation of Christianity,' I may, I trust without offense, persuade myself that thousands of our fathers in former times, living and dying within her walls, have found mercy at the hands of God.

What although they repented not of their errors? God for-

bid that I should open my mouth to gainsay that which
Christ himself hath spoken: 'Except ye repent, ye shall all
perish.'[56] And if they did not repent they perished. But
withal note that we have the benefit of a double repentence.
The least sin which we commit in deed, work, or thought is
dead, without repentance. Yet how many things do escape
us in every of these which we do not know, how many which
we do not observe to be sins! And without the knowledge,
without the observation of sin there is no actual repentance. It cannot then be chosen but that for as many as hold
the foundation, and have all known sin and error in hatred,
the blessing of repentance for unknown sins and errors is
obtained at the hands of God through the gracious media-
tion of Christ Jesus, for such suitors as cry with the prophet
David, 'Purge me, O Lord, from my secret sins.'[57]

But we wash a wall of loam; we labour in vain; all this is
nothing; it doth not prove, it cannot justify, that which we
go about to maintain. Infidels and heathen men are not so
godless but that they may, no doubt, cry God mercy, and
desire in general to have their sins forgiven them. To such
as deny the foundation of faith there can be no salvation,
according to the ordinary course which God doth use in
saving men, without a particular repentance of that error.
The Galatians, thinking that except they were circumcised
they could not be saved, otherthrew the foundation of faith
directly. Therefore if any of them did die so persuaded,
whether before or after they were told of their error, their
case is dreadful; there is no way with them but one, death
and condemnation. For the Apostle speaketh nothing of
men departed, but saith generally of all: 'If ye be circumcised Christ shall profit you nothing. Ye are abolished from
Christ, whosoever are justified by the law; ye are fallen from
grace.'[58] Of them in the Church of Rome the reason is the
same. For whom Antichrist hath seduced, concerning them
did not St. Paul speak long before, that 'because they received not the love of the truth that they might be saved,
therefore would God send them strong delusions to believe
lies, that all they might be damned who believed not the
truth but had pleasure in unrighteousness'?[59] And St. John:
'all that dwell upon the earth shall worship him,[60] whose
names are not written in the Book of Life.'[61] Indeed many of
them in former times, as their books and writings do yet

show, held the foundation, to wit, salvation by Christ alone, and therefore might be saved. For God hath always had a Church among them who firmly kept his saving truth. As for such as hold with the Church of Rome that we cannot be saved by Christ alone without works, they do not only by a circle of consequence, but directly, deny the foundation of faith; they hold it not, not so much as by a slender thread.

General repentance not intended

This, to my remembrance, being all that hath been as yet opposed with any countenance or show of reason, I hope, if this be answered, the cause in question is at an end. Concerning general repentance, therefore: what? a murderer, a blasphemer, an unclean person, a Turk, a Jew, any sinner to escape the wrath of God by a general 'God forgive me'? Truly, it never came within my heart that a general repentance doth serve for all sins or for all sinners: it serveth only for the common oversights of our sinful life, and for faults which either we do not mark, or do not know that they are faults. Our fathers were actually penitent for sins wherein they knew they displeased God, or else they come not within the compass of my first speech. Again, that otherwise they could not be saved than holding the foundation of Christian faith, we have not only affirmed but proved. Why is it not then confessed that thousands of our fathers, although they lived in popish superstitions, might yet, by the mercy of God, be saved? First, if they had directly denied the very foundation of Christianity, without repenting them particularly of that sin, he who saith there could be no salvation for them, according to the ordinary course which God doth use in saving men, granteth plainly, or at the leastwise closely insinuateth, that an extraordinary privilege of mercy might deliver their souls from hell; which is more than I required. Secondly, if the foundation be denied, it is denied by force of some heresy which the Church of Rome maintaineth. But how many were there amongst our fathers who, being seduced by the common error of that church, never knew the meaning of her heresies! So that if all popish heretics did perish, thousands of them who lived in popish superstitions might be saved.

Thirdly, seeing all that held popish heresies did not hold

Thirdly, seeing all that held popish heresies did not hold all the heresies of the pope, why might not thousands who were infected with other leaven live and die unsoured by this, and so be saved? Fourthly, if they all had held this heresy, many there were that held it no doubt only in a general form of words, which a favourable interpreter might expound in a sense differing far enough from the poisoned conceit of heresy; as, for example: did they hold that we cannot be saved by Christ without works? We ourselves do, I think, all say as much, with this construction, salvation being taken as in that sentence, 'With the heart man believes unto justification and with the mouth confession is made unto salvation.'[62] Except infants, and men cut off upon the point of their conversion, of the rest none shall see God but such as seek peace and holiness, though not as a cause of their salvation, yet as a way through which they must walk that will be saved. Did they hold that without works we are not justified? Take justification so that it may also imply sanctification, and St. James doth say as much; for except there be an ambiguity in some term, St. Paul and St. James do contradict each other; which cannot be. Now, there is no ambiguity in the name either of faith or of works, both being meant by them both in one and the same sense. Finding therefore that justification is spoken of by St. Paul without implying sanctification when he proveth that a man is justified by faith without works; finding likewise that justification doth sometimes imply sanctification also with it; I suppose nothing more sound than so to interpret St. James as speaking not in that sense, but in this.

We have already showed that there are two kinds of Christian righteousness: the one without us, which we have by imputation; the other in us, which consisteth of faith, hope, charity, and other Christian virtues; and St. James doth prove that Abraham had not only the one, because the thing he believed was imputed unto him for righteousness, but also the other, because he offered up his son. God giveth us both the one justice[63] and the other: the one by accepting us for righteous in Christ; the other by working Christian righteousness in us. The proper and most immediate efficient cause in us of this latter is the spirit of adoption which we have received into our hearts.[64] That whereof if consisteth,

whereof it is really and formally made, are those infused virtues proper and particular unto saints, which the Spirit, in
that very moment when first it is given of God, bringeth with
it. The effects thereof are such actions as the Apostle doth
call the fruits, the works, the operations of the Spirit;[65] the
difference of which operations, from the root whereof they
spring, maketh it needful to put two kinds likewise of sanctifying righteousness, habitual and actual: habitual, that
holiness wherewith our souls are inwardly endued the same
instant when first we begin to be temples of the Holy
Ghost;[66] actual, that holiness which afterward beautifieth
all the parts and actions of our life, the holiness for which
Enoch, Job, Zachary, Elizabeth, and other saints are in
Scriptures so highly commended.[67]

If here it be demanded which of these we do first receive,
I answer that the Spirit, the virtues of the Spirit, the habitual
justice which is ingrafted, the external justice of Christ Jesus
which is imputed, these we receive all at one and the same
time. Whensoever we have any of these we have all; they go
together. Yet since no man is justified except he believe,
and no man believeth except he have faith, and no man hath
faith unless he have received the Spirit of adoption, forasmuch as these do necessarily infer justification, but justification doth of necessity presuppose them; we must needs
hold that imputed righteousness, in dignity being the chiefest, is notwithstanding in order the last of all these,[68] but
actual righteousness, which is the righteousness of good
works, succeedeth all, followeth after all, both in order and
in time. Which thing being attentively marked showeth
plainly how the faith of true believers cannot be divorced
from hope and love; how faith is a part of sanctification, and
yet unto sanctification necessary; how faith is perfected by
good works, and yet no works of ours good without faith;
finally, how our fathers might hold, we are justified by faith
alone, and yet hold truly that without good works we are not
justified. Did they think that men do merit rewards in heaven
by the works they perform on earth? The ancient fathers use
meriting for *obtaining,* and in that sense they of Wittenberg
have in their Confession: 'We teach that good works commanded of God are necessarily to be done, and that by the
free kindness of God they merit their certain rewards.'[69] Others
therefore, speaking as our fathers did, and we taking their

speech in a sound meaning, as we may take our fathers',
and ought, forasmuch as their meaning is doubtful and
charity doth always interpret doubtful things favourably,
what should induce us to think that rather the damage of
the worse construction did light upon them all than that the
blessing of the better was granted unto thousands?

Fifthly, if in the worst construction that can be made they
had all embraced it living, might not many of them dying
utterly renounce it? Howsoever men, when they sit at ease,
do vainly tickle their own hearts with the wanton conceit of
I know not what proportionable correspondence between
their merits and their rewards, which, in the trance of their
high speculations, they dream that God hath measured,
weighed, and laid up, as it were, in bundles for them; notwithstanding we see by daily experience, in a number even
of them, that when the hour of death approacheth, when
they secretly hear themselves summoned forthwith to appear and stand at the bar of that Judge whose brightness
causeth the eyes of angels themselves to dazzle, all those
idle imaginations do then begin to hide their faces. To name
merits then is to lay their souls upon the rack; the memory
of their own deeds is loathsome unto them; they forsake all
things wherein they have put any trust and confidence: no
staff to lean upon, no ease, no rest, no comfort then, but
only in Christ Jesus.

Wherefore if this proposition were true, 'To hold in such
wise as the Church of Rome doth that we cannot be saved by
Christ alone without works is directly to deny the foundation of faith' — I say that if this proposition were true, nevertheless so many ways I have showed whereby we may hope
that thousands of our fathers living in popish superstitions
might be saved. But what if it be not true? What if neither
that of the Galatians concerning circumcision nor this of
the Church of Rome about works be any direct denial of the
foundation, as it is affirmed that both are? I need not wade
so far as to discuss this controversy, the matter which first
was brought into question being so cleared, as I hope it is.
Howbeit, because I desire that the truth even in this also
may receive light, I will do mine endeavour to set down
somewhat more plainly, first, the foundation of faith, what
it is; secondly, what it is directly to deny the foundation;
thirdly, whether they whom God hath chosen to be heirs of

life may fall so far as directly to deny it; fourthly, whether the Galatians did so by admitting the error about circumcision and the law; last of all, whether the Church of Rome, for this one opinion of works, may be thought to do the like, and thereupon to be no more a Christian Church than are the assemblies of Turks or Jews.

This word *foundation* being figuratively used hath always reference to somewhat which resembleth a material building, as both the doctrine of Christianity and the community of Christians do. By the masters of civil policy nothing is so much inculcated as that commonwealths are founded upon laws; for that a multitude cannot be compacted into one body otherwise than by a common acceptation of laws, whereby they are to be kept in order. The ground of all civil laws is this: No man ought to be hurt or injured by another. Take away this persuasion and you take away all laws; take away laws, and what shall become of commonwealths? So it is in our spiritual Christian community: I do not now mean that body mystical whereof Christ is the only head, that building undiscernible by mortal eyes wherein Christ is the chief cornerstone;[70] but I speak of the visible church, the foundation whereof is the doctrine of the prophets and apostles professed.[71] The mark whereunto their doctrine tendeth is pointed at in those words of Peter unto Christ, 'Thou has the words of eternal life';[72] in those of Paul to Timothy, 'The Holy Scriptures are able to make thee wise unto salvation.'[73]

It is the demand of nature itself: 'What shall we do to have eternal life?'[74] The desire of immortality and of the knowledge of that whereby it may be attained is so natural unto all men that even they who are not persuaded that they shall do notwithstanding wish that they might know a way how to see no end of life. And because natural means are not able still to resist the force of death, there is no people in the earth so savage which hath not devised some supernatural help or other to fly unto for aid and succour in extremities against the enemies of their lives. A longing therefore to be saved, without understanding the true way how, hath been the cause of all the superstitions in the world. O that the miserable estate of others, who wander in darkness and wot not whither they go, could give us understanding hearts worthily to esteem the riches of the mercies of God towards us, before whose eyes the doors of the kingdom of heaven are set wide open! Should we not offer violence unto it? It offereth violence to us, and we gather strength to withstand it.

The ground of salvation

But I am besides my purpose when I fall to bewail the cold affection which we bear towards that whereby we should be saved, my purpose being only to set down what the ground of salvation is. The doctrine of the Gospel proposeth salvation as the end, and doth it not teach the way of attaining thereunto? Yes, the damsel possessed with a spirit of divination spake the truth: 'These men are the servants of the most high God who show unto us the way of salvation'[76] — 'a new and living way which Christ hath prepared for us through the veil, that is, his flesh,'[77] salvation purchased by the death of Christ. By this foundation the children of God, before the time of the written law, were distinguished from the sons of men. The reverend patriarchs both professed it living and spake expressly of it in the hour of their death.[78] It comforted Job in the midst of grief.[79] It was afterwards likewise the anchor-hold of all the righteous in Israel, from the writing of the law to the time of grace; every prophet maketh mention of it.[80] It was so famously spoken of about the time when the coming of Christ to accomplish the promises, which were made long before, drew near, that the sound thereof was heard even amongst the Gentiles.[81] When he was come, as many as were his acknowledged that he was their salvation; he, that long-expected hope of Israel; he, that 'seed in whom all the nations of the world should be blessed.'[82] So that now his name is a name of ruin, a name of death and condemnation, unto such as dream of a new Messiah, to as many as look for salvation by any other than by him: 'For amongst men there is given no other name under heaven whereby we must be saved.'[83] Thus much St. Mark doth intimate by that which he putteth in the very front of his book, making his entrance with these words: 'The beginning of the Gospel of Jesus Christ, the Son of God.' His doctrine he termeth the Gospel because it teacheth salvation; the Gospel of Jesus Christ, the Son of God, because it teacheth salvation by him.

This is then the foundation whereupon the frame of the Gospel is erected; that very Jesus whom the Virgin conceived of the Holy Ghost, whom Simeon embraced in his arms,[84] whom Pilate condemned, whom the Jews crucified, whom the Apostles preached, he is Christ, the Lord, the only Saviour of the world: 'other foundation can no man lay.'[85] Thus I have briefly opened that principle in Christianity which we call the foundation of our faith. It followeth now that I declare unto you what it is directly to overthrow it. This will better appear if first we understand what it is to hold the foundation of faith.

There are who defend that many of the Gentiles who never heard the name of Christ held the foundation of Christianity: and why? They acknowledged many of them the providence of God, his infinite wisdom, strength, and power, his goodness and his mercy towards the children of men; that God hath judgment in store for the wicked, but for the righteous that seek him rewards, etc. In this which they confessed that lieth covered which we believe; in the rudiments of their knowledge concerning God the foundation of our faith concerning Christ lieth secretly wrapped up and is virtually contained: therefore they hold the foundation of faith, though they never heard it. Might we not with as good colour of reason defend that every ploughman hath all the sciences wherein philosphers have excelled? For no man is ignorant of the first principles which do virtually contain whatsoever by natural means either is or can be known. Yea, might we not with as good reason affirm that a man may put three mighty oaks wheresoever three acorns may be put? For virtually an acorn is an oak. To avoid such paradoxes, we teach plainly that to hold the foundation is in express terms to acknowledge it.

Now, because the foundation is an affirmative proposition, they all overthrow it who deny it; they directly overthrow it who deny it directly; and they overthrow it by consequent, or indirectly, who hold any one assertion whatsoever whereupon the direct denial thereof may be necessarily concluded. What is the question between the Gentiles and us but this: whether salvation be by Christ? What between the Jews and us but this: whether by this Jesus whom we call Christ, yea or no? This to be the main point whereupon Christianity standeth, it is clear by that one sentence of

Festus concerning Paul's accusers: 'They brought no crime of such things as I supposed, but had certain questions against him of their own superstition, and of one Jesus who was dead, whom Paul affirmed to be alive.'[86] Where we see that Jesus, dead and raised for the salvation of the world, is by Jews denied, despised by a Gentile, and by a Christian apostle maintained. The fathers therefore in the primitive Church when they wrote—Tertullian, the book which he calleth *Apologeticus;* Minucius Felix, the book which he entitleth *Octavius;* Arnobius, his seven books against the Gentiles; Chrysostom, his orations against the Jews; Eusebius, his ten books of evangelical demonstration—they stood in defence of Christianity against them by whom the foundation thereof was directly denied. But the writings of the fathers against Novatians, Pelagians, and other heretics of the like note, refel[87] positions whereby the foundation of Christian faith was overthrown by consequent only. In the former sort of writings the foundation is proved; in the latter it is alleged as a proof, which to men that had been known directly to deny it must needs have seemed a very beggarly kind of disputing. All infidels therefore deny the foundation of faith directly. By consequent, many a Christian man, yea whole Christian churches, have denied it and do deny it at this present day. Christian churches denying the foundation of Christianity? Not directly, for then they cease to be Christian churches; but by consequent, in respect whereof we condemn them as erroneous, although for holding the foundation we do and must hold them Christian.

We see what it is to hold the foundation; what directly and what by consequent to deny it. The next thing which followeth is whether they whom God hath chosen to obtain the glory of our Lord Jesus Christ may, being once effectually called, and through faith truly justified, afterwards fall so far as directly to deny the foundation which their hearts have before embraced with joy and comfort in the Holy Ghost, for such is the faith which indeed doth justify. Devils know the same things which we believe,[88] and the minds of the most ungodly may be fully persuaded of the truth, which knowledge in the one and persuasion in the other is sometimes termed faith, but equivocally, being indeed no such faith as that whereby a Christian man is justified. It is the spirit of adoption which worketh faith in us, in them not. The things which we believe are by us apprehended not only as true but also as good, and that to us: as good, they are not by them apprehended; as true, they are.

Whereupon followeth a third difference: the Christian man the more he increaseth in faith the more his joy and comfort aboundeth; but they, the more sure they are of the truth, the more they quake and tremble at it. This begetteth another effect, wherein the hearts of the one sort have a different disposition from the other. 'I am not ignorant,' saith Minucius, 'that there are too many who, being conscious what they are to look for, do rather wish that they might than think that they shall cease to be when they cease to live; because they hold it better that death should consume them unto nothing than God receive them unto punishment.'[89] So it is in other articles of faith, whereof wicked men think, no doubt, many times they are too true. On the contrary side, to the other there is no grief nor torment greater than to feel their persuasion weak in things whereof, when they are persuaded, they reap such comfort and joy of spirit; such is the faith whereby we are justified—such, I mean, in respect of the quality. For touching the principal object of faith, longer than it holdeth that foundation whereof we have spoken it neither justifieth, nor is, but ceaseth to be faith when it ceaseth to believe that Jesus Christ is the only Saviour of the world.

The cause of life spiritual in us is Christ, not carnally or corporally inhabiting, but dwelling in the soul of man, as a thing which (when the mind apprehendeth it) is said to inhabit and possess the mind. The mind conceiveth Christ by hearing the doctrine of Christianity. As the light of nature doth cause the mind to apprehend those truths which are merely rational, so that saving truth, which is far above the reach of human reason, cannot otherwise than by the Spirit of the Almighty be conceived. All these are implied wheresoever any one of them is mentioned as the cause of spiritual life. Wherefore when we read that 'the Spirit is our life,'[90] or 'the Word our life,'[91] or 'Christ our life,'[92] we are in every of these to understand that our life is Christ, by the hearing of the Gospel apprehended as a Saviour, and assented unto by the power of the Holy Ghost. The first intellectual conceit and comprehension of Christ so embraced St. Peter calleth the seed whereof we be new born.[93] Our first embracing of Christ is our first reviving from the state of death and condemnation.[94] 'He that hath the Son hath life,' saith St. John, 'and he that hath not the Son of God hath not life.'[95] If therefore he who once hath the Son may cease to have the Son, though it be but a moment, he ceaseth for that moment to have life. But the life of them who live by the Son of God is everlasting, not only for that it shall be everlasting in the world to come, but because, as 'Christ being raised from the dead dieth no more, death hath no more power over him,'[96] so the justified man, being alive to God in Jesus Christ our Lord, by whom he hath life, liveth always.[97]

Eternal security in Christ

I might, if I had not otherwhere largely done it already, show by sundry manifest and clear proofs how the motions and operations of life are sometimes so undiscernible and secret, that they seem stone-dead who notwithstanding are still alive unto God in Christ.

For as long as that abideth in us which animateth, quickeneth, and giveth life, so long we live; and we know that the cause of our life abideth in us for ever. If Christ, the fountain of life, may flit and leave the habitation where once he dwelleth, what shall become of his promise, 'I am with you to the world's end'? [98] If the seed of God, which containeth Christ, may be first conceived and then cast out, how doth St. Peter term it immortal?[99] How doth St. John affirm it abideth?[100] If the Spirit, which is given to cherish and preserve the seed of life, may be given and taken away, how is it the earnest of our inheritance until redemption,[101] how doth it continue with us for ever?[102] If therefore the man who is once just by faith shall live by faith and live for ever, it followeth that he who once doth believe the foundation must needs believe the foundation for ever. If he believe it for ever, how can he ever directly deny it? Faith holding the direct affirmation, the direct negation, so long as faith continueth, is excluded.

But ye will say that, as he who today is holy may tomorrow forsake his holiness and become impure, as a friend may change his mind and become an enemy, as hope may wither, so faith may die in the heart of man, the Spirit may be quenched,[103] grace may be extinguished, they who believe may be quite turned away from the truth. The case is clear, long experience hath made this manifest, it needs no proof.

I grant that we are apt, prone, and ready to forsake God; but is God as ready to forsake us? Our minds are changeable; is his so likewise? Whom God hath justified hath not Christ assured that it is his Father's will to give them a kingdom?[104] Which kingdom, notwithstanding, shall not otherwise be given them than 'if they continue grounded and established in the faith and be not moved away from the hope of the Gospel',[105] 'if they abide in love and holiness.'[106] Our Saviour therefore, when he spake of the sheep effectually called and truly gathered into his fold, 'I give unto them eternal life and they shall never perish, neither shall any pluck them out of my hand,'[107] in promising to save them, promised, no doubt, to preserve them in that without which there can be no salvation, as also from that whereby salvation is irremediably lost. Every error in things appertaining to God is repugnant unto faith; every fearful cogitation, unto hope; unto love, every straggling inordinate desire; unto holiness, every blemish whereby either the inward thoughts of our minds or the outward actions of our lives are stained. But heresy, such as that of Ebion, Cerinthus, and others, against whom the Apostles were forced to bend themselves, both by word and also by writing; that repining discouragement of heart which tempteth God, whereof we have Israel in the desert for a pattern;[108] coldness, such as that in the angel of Ephesus;[109] foul sins known to be expressly against the first or the second table of the law, such as Noah, Manasses, David, Solomon, and Peter committed: these are each in their kind so opposite to the former virtues that they leave no place for salvation without an actual repentance. But infidelity, extreme despair, hatred of God and all godliness, obduration in sin, cannot stand where there is the least spark of faith, hope, love, or sanctity, even as cold in the lowest degree cannot be where heat in the first degree is found.

Whereupon I conclude that, although in the first kind no man liveth that sinneth not, and in, the second, as perfect as any do live may sin, yet since the man who is born of God hath a promise that in him the seed of God shall abide,[110] which seed is a sure preservative against the sins of the third suit, greater and clearer assurance we cannot have of

anything than of this, that from such sins God shall preserve the righteous, as the apple of his eye, for ever.[111]
Directly we deny the foundation of faith, is plain infidelity.
Where faith is entered, there infidelity is for ever excluded.
Therefore by him who hath once sincerely believed in Christ
the foundation of Christian faith can never be directly
denied. Did not Peter,[112] did not Marcellinus,[113] did not many
others both directly deny Christ after they had believed and
again believe after they had denied? No doubt, as they may
confess in word whose condemnation nevertheless is their
not believing (for example we have Judas), so likewise they
may believe in heart whose condemnation, without repentance, is their not confessing. Although therefore Peter and
the rest, for whose faith Christ had prayed that it might not
fail,[114] did not by denial sin the sin of infidelity, which is an
inward abnegation of Christ (for if they had done this their
faith had clearly failed); yet, because they sinned notoriously
and grievously, committing that which they knew to be so
expressly forbidden by the law, which saith, 'thou shalt worship the Lord thy God and him only shalt thou serve,'[115] necessary it was that he who purposed to save their souls should,
as he did, touch their hearts with true unfeigned repentance, that his mercy might restore them again to life whom
sin had made the children of death and condemnation.

Touching this point, therefore, I hope I may safely set it
down that if the justified err, as he may, and never come to
understand his error, God doth save him through general
repentance; but if he fall into heresy, he calleth him either
at one time or other by actual repentance; but from infidelity,
which is an inward direct denial of the foundation, preserveth him by special providence for ever. Whereby we may
easily know what to think of those Galatians whose hearts
were so possessed with love of the truth that, if it had been
possible, they would have plucked out their very eyes to
bestow upon their teachers.[116] It is true that they were afterwards greatly changed, both in persuasion and affection, so
that the Galatians, when St. Paul wrote unto them, were not
now the Galatians which they had been in former times, for
that through error they wandered, although they were his
sheep.[117] I do not deny, but I should deny that they were his
sheep, if I should grant that through error they perished. It
was a perilous opinion which they held, in them who held it

only as an error, because it overthroweth the foundation by consequent. But in them who obstinately maintained it I cannot think it less than a damnable heresy.

Distinctions to be made

We must therefore put a difference between them who err of ignorance, retaining nevertheless a mind desirous to be instructed in the truth, and them who, after the truth is laid open, persist in stubborn defence of their blindness. Heretical defenders, froward and stiffnecked teachers of circumcision, the blessed Apostle calleth dogs.[118] Silly men, that were seduced to think they taught the truth, he pitieth, he taketh up in his arms, he lovingly embraceth, he kisseth, and with more than fatherly tenderness doth so temper, qualify, and correct the speech he useth towards them, that a man cannot easily discern whether did most abound, the love which he bare to their godly affection or the grief which the danger of their opinion bred him. Their opinion was dangerous; was not so likewise theirs who thought that the kingdom of Christ should be earthly? was not theirs who thought that the Gospel should be preached only to the Jews? What more opposite to prophetical doctrine concerning the coming of Christ than the one, concerning the Catholic Church than the other? Yet they who had these fancies, even when they had them, were not the worst men in the world. The heresy of freewill was a millstone about the Pelagians' neck: shall we therefore give sentence of death inevitable against all those fathers in the Greek church who, being mispersuaded, died in the error of freewill?

Of those Galatians, therefore, who first were justified, and then deceived, as I can see no cause why as many as died before admonition might not by mercy be saved, even in error, so I make no doubt but as many as lived till they were admonished found the mercy of God effectual in converting them from their error, lest any one that is Christ's should perish. Of this, as I take it, there is no controversy. Only against the salvation of them who died, though before admonition, yet in error, it is objected that their opinion was a very plain direct denial of the foundation. If Paul and Barnabas had been so persuaded, they would haply have used their terms otherwise, speaking of the masters themselves

who did first set that error abroach, 'certain of the sect of
the Pharisees who believed.'[119] What difference was there
between these Pharisees and others from whom by a special
description they are distinguished but this: they who came
to Antioch teaching the necessity of circumcision were
Christians, the other, enemies of Christianity? Why then
should these be termed so distinctly believers, if they did
directly deny the foundation of our belief, besides which
there was none other thing that made the rest to be
unbelievers?

We need go no further than St. Paul's very reasoning
against them for proof of this matter: 'Seeing ye know God,
or rather are known of God, how turn you again unto impo-
tent rudiments? The law engendereth servants, her children are in bondage. They who are begotten by the Gospel
are free. Brethren, we are not children of the servant, but of
the free woman, and will ye yet be under the law?'[120] That
they thought it unto salvation necessary for the Church of
Christ to observe days and months and times and years, to
keep the ceremonies and the sacraments of the law, this
was their error.[121] Yet he who condemneth their error confesseth, notwithstanding, that they knew God and were
known of him; he taketh not the honour from them to be
termed sons begotten of the immortal seed of the Gospel.
Let the heaviest words which he useth be weighed; consider
the drift of these dreadful conclusions: 'If ye be circumcised, Christ shall profit you nothing; as many as are justified by the law, ye are fallen from grace.'[122] It had been to no
purpose in the world so to urge them had not the Apostle
been persuaded that at the hearing of such sequels, 'no
benefit by Christ,' 'a defection from grace,' their hearts
would tremble and quake within them; and why? because
they knew that in Christ, in grace, their salvation lay, which
is a plain direct acknowledgement of the foundation.

Lest I should herein seem to hold that which no one godly
and learned hath done, let these words be considered,
which import as much as I affirm: 'Surely those brethren
who, in St. Paul's time, thought that God did lay a necessity
upon them to make choice of days and meats spake as they
believed, and could not but in words condemn that liberty
which they supposed to be brought in against the authority
of divine Scripture. Otherwise it had been needless for St.

Paul to admonish them not to condemn such as eat without scrupulosity whatsoever was set before them. This error, if ye weigh what it is of itself, did at once overthrow all Scripture whereby we are taught salvation by faith in Christ, all that ever the prophets did foretell, all that ever the Apostles did preach of Christ. It drew with it the denial of Christ entirely, insomuch that St. Paul complaineth that his labour was lost upon the Galatians, unto whom this error was obtruded, affirming that Christ, if so be they were circumcised, should not profit them anything at all. Yet so far was St. Paul from striking their names out of Christ's book that he commanded others to entertain them, to accept them with singular humanity, to use them like brethren. He knew men's imbecility, he had a feeling of our blindness who are mortal men how great it is, and being sure that they are the sons of God whosoever he endued with his fear would not have them counted enemies of that whereunto they could not as yet frame themselves to be friends, but did even of a very religious affection to the truth unwittingly reject and resist the truth. They acknowledged Christ to be their only and their perfect Saviour, but saw not how repugnant their believing the necessity of Mosaical ceremonies was to their faith in Jesus Christ.'[123]

Hereunto reply is made that if they had not directly denied the foundation they might have been saved; but saved they could not be; therefore their opinion was, not only by consequent, but directly, a denial of the foundation. When the question was about the possibility of their salvation, their denying of the foundation was brought for proof that they could not be saved: now that the question is about their denial, the impossibility of their salvation is alleged to prove they denied the foundation. Is there nothing which excludeth men from salvation but only the foundation of faith denied? I should have thought that, beside this, many other things are death except they be actually repented of, as indeed this opinion of theirs was death unto as many as, being given to understand that to cleave thereunto was to fall from Christ, did notwithstanding cleave unto it. But of this enough. Wherefore I come to the last question: whether the doctrine of the Church of Rome concerning the necessity of works unto salvation be a direct denial of the foundation of our faith.

Rome and the necessity of works

I seek not to obtrude upon you any private opinions of mine own. The best learned in our profession are of this judgment, that all the heresies and corruptions of the Church of Rome do not prove her to deny the foundation directly. If they did, they should prove her simply to be no Christian Church. 'But I suppose,' saith one, 'that in the papacy some church remaineth, a church crazed, or, if you will, broken quite in pieces, forlorn, misshapen, yet some church.' His reason is this: 'Antichrist must sit in the temple of God.'[124] Lest any man should think such sentences as this to be true only in regard of them whom that church is supposed to have kept by the special providence of God, as it were in the secret corners of his bosom, free from infection and as sound in the faith as, we trust, by his mercy we ourselves are, I permit it to your wise considerations whether it be not more likely that, as phrensy, though itself take away the use of reason, doth notwithstanding prove them reasonable creatures who have it, because none can be frantic but they, so antichristianity, being the bane and plain overthrow of Christianity, may nevertheless argue the church wherein Antichrist sitteth to be Christian. Neither have I ever hitherto heard or read any one word alleged of force to warrant that God doth otherwise than, so as hath been in the next two questions before declared, bind himself to keep his elect from worshipping the beast and from receiving his mark in their foreheads;[125] but he hath preserved and will preserve them from receiving any deadly wound at the hands of the man of sin, whose deceit hath prevailed over none to death but only such as never loved the truth and such as took pleasure in unrighteousness. They, in all ages, whose hearts have delighted in the principal truth and whose souls have thirsted after righteousness, if they received the mark of error, the mercy of God, even erring and dangerously erring, might save them; if they received the mark of heresy, the same mercy did, I doubt not, convert them.

How far Romish heresies may prevail over God's elect, how many God hath kept from falling into them, how many have been converted from them, is not the question now in hand; for if heaven had not received any one of that coat for these thousand years it may still be true that the doctrine which at this day they do profess doth not directly deny the foundation and so prove them to be no Christian Church. One I have alleged whose words, in my ears, sound that way.[126] Shall I add another whose speech is plainer? 'I deny her not the name of a church', saith another, 'no more than to a man the name of a man as long as he liveth, what sickness soever he hath.' His reason is this: 'Salvation in Jesus Christ, which is the mark joineth the Head with the body, Jesus Christ with his church, it is so cut off by man's merits, by the merits of saints, by the pope's pardons, and such other wickedness that the life of the Church holdeth by a very little thread';[127] yet still the life of the Church holdeth. A third hath these words: 'I acknowledge the church of Rome, even at this present day, for a church of Christ, such a church as Israel under Jeroboam, yet a church'. His reason is this: 'Every man seeth, except he willingly hoodwink himself, that as always so now the church of Rome holdeth firmly and steadfastly the doctrine of truth concerning God and the person of our Lord Jesus Christ, and baptizeth in the name of the Father, the Son, and the Holy Ghost, confesseth and avoucheth Christ for the only Redeemer of the world and the Judge that shall sit upon quick and dead, receiving true believers into endless joy, faithless and godless men being cast with Satan and his angels into flames unquenchable'.[128]

I may, and will rein the question shorter than they do. Let the pope take down his top and captivate no more men's souls by his papal jurisdiction; let him no longer count himself lord paramount over the princes of the earth, no longer use kings as his tenants *paravaile*;[129] let his stately senate submit their necks to the yoke of Christ and cease to dye their garments, like Edom, in blood; let them, from the highest to the lowest, hate and foresake their idolatry, abjure all their errors and heresies wherewith they have perverted the truth; let them strip their church till they have no polluted rag but this one about her: 'By Christ alone, without works, we cannot be saved.' It is enough for me if I show that the holding of this one thing doth not prove the foundation of faith directly denied in the Church of Rome.

Works are an addition to the foundation. Be it so, what then? The foundation is not subverted by every kind of addition. Simply to add unto those fundamental words is not to

mingle wine with puddle, heaven with earth, things polluted
with the sanctified blood of Christ: of which crime indict
them who attribute those operations, in whole or in part, to
any creature which in the work of our salvation are wholly
peculiar unto Christ; and if I open my mouth to speak in
their defence, if I hold my peace and plead not against them
as long as breath is in my body, let me be guilty of all the
dishonour that ever hath been done to the Son of God. But
the more dreadful a thing it is to deny salvation by Christ
alone, the more slow and fearful I am, except it be too manifest to lay a thing so grievous unto any man's charge. Let us
beware lest, if we make too many ways of denying Christ, we
scarce leave any way for ourselves truly and soundly to confess him. Salvation only by Christ is the true foundation
whereupon indeed Christianity standeth. But what if I say,
'Ye cannot be saved only by Christ without this addition:
Christ believed in heart, confessed with mouth, obeyed in
life and conversation'? Because I add, do I therefore deny
that which directly I did affirm? There may be an addita-
ment of explication which overthroweth not but proveth
and concludeth the proposition whereunto it is annexed. He
that saith Peter was a chief apostle doth prove that Peter
was an apostle.[130] He who saith our salvation is of the Lord,
through sanctification of the Spirit and faith of the truth,[131]
proveth that our salvation is of the Lord. But if that which is
added be such a privation as taketh away the very essence
of that whereunto it is adjoined, then by sequel it overthroweth. In like sort, he that should say, 'Our election is of
grace for our works' sake,' should then grant in sound of
words, but indeed by consequent deny, that our election is
of grace; for the grace which electeth us is no grace if it elect
us for our works' sake.

Now whereas the Church of Rome addeth works, we must
note, further, that the adding works is not like the adding of
circumcision unto Christ. Christ came not to abrogate and
take away good works: he did, to change circumcision; for
we see that in place thereof he hath substituted holy baptism. To say, 'Ye cannot be saved by Christ except ye be circumcised', is to add a thing excluded, a thing not only not
necessary to be kept, but necessary not to be kept by them
that will be saved. On the other side, to say, 'Ye cannot be
saved by Christ without works,' is to add things not only not

excluded, but commanded, as being in place and in their kind necessary, and therefore subordinated unto Christ, even by Christ himself, by whom the web of salvation is spun: 'Except your righteousness exceed the righteousness of the scribes and Pharisees, ye shall not enter into the kingdom of heaven.'[132] They were rigorous exacters of things not utterly to be neglected and left undone, washings and tithings, etc.[133] As they were in these things, so must we be in judgment and the love of God. Christ, in works ceremonial, giveth more liberty, in moral, much less, than they did.[134] Works of righteousness therefore are not so repugnantly added in the one proposition as in the other circumcision is.

Faith does not exclude works

But we say our salvation is by Christ alone; therefore howsoever or whatsoever we add unto Christ in the matter of salvation we overthrow Christ. Our case were very hard if this argument, so universally meant as it is proposed, were sound and good. We ourselves do not teach Christ alone, excluding our own faith, unto justification, Christ alone, excluding our own works, unto sanctification, Christ alone, excluding the one or the other as unnecessary unto salvation. It is a childish cavil wherewith in the matter of justification our adversaries do so greatly please themselves, exclaiming that we tread all Christian virtues under our feet and require nothing in Christians but faith, because we teach that faith alone justifieth; whereas by this speech we never meant to exclude either hope and charity from being always joined as inseparable mates with faith in the man that is justified, or works from being added as necessary duties, required at the hands of every justified man, but to show that faith is the only hand which putteth on Christ unto justification, and Christ the only garment which, being so put on, covereth the shame of our defiled natures, hideth the imperfections of our works, preserveth us blameless in the sight of God, before whom otherwise the very weakness of our faith were cause sufficient to make us culpable, yea, to shut us out from the kingdom of heaven, where nothing that is not absolute can enter.

That our dealing with them be not childish as theirs with

us when we hear of salvation by Christ alone, considering
that ('alone' is an) exclusive particle, we are to note what it
doth exclude, and where. If I say, 'Such a judge only ought
to determine such a cause,' all things incident unto the
determination thereof besides the person of the judge, as
laws, depositions, evidences, etc., are not hereby excluded;
persons are, yet not from witnessing herein or assisting,
but only from determining and giving sentence. How then is
our salvation wrought by Christ alone? Is it our meaning
that nothing is requisite to man's salvation but Christ to
save, and he to be saved quietly without any more to do? No,
we acknowledge no such foundation. As we have received,
so we teach that besides the bare and naked work wherein
Christ, without any other associate, finished all the parts of
our redemption and purchased salvation himself alone, for
conveyance of this eminent blessing unto us many things
are required, as to be known and chosen of God before the
foundation of the world, in the world to be called, justified,
sanctified, after we have left the world to be received into
glory: Christ in every one of these hath something which he
worketh alone. Through him, according to the eternal purpose of God before the foundation of the world, born, crucified, buried, raised, etc., we were in a gracious acceptation
known unto God long before we were seen of men: God knew
us, loved us, was kind towards us in Christ Jesus; in him he
we were elected to be heirs of life.[135]

Thus far God through Christ hath wrought in such sort
alone that ourselves are mere patients, working no more
than dead and senseless matter, wood or stone or iron, doth
in the artificer's hand, no more than the clay when the potter
appointeth it to be framed for an honourable use; nay, not
so much. For the matter whereupon the craftsman worketh
he chooseth, being moved by the fitness which is in it to
serve his turn; in us no such thing. Touching the rest, that
which is laid for the foundation of our faith importeth, further, that by him we be called, that we have redemption,
remission of sins through his blood, health by his stripes,
justice by him; that he doth sanctify his Church and make it
glorious to himself; that entrance into joy shall be given us
by him; yea, all things by him alone. Howbeit, not so by him
alone as if in us, to our vocation, the hearing of the Gospel;
to our justification, faith; to our santification, the fruits of

the Spirit; to our entrance into rest, perseverance in hope, in faith, in holiness, were not necessary.

Then what is the fault of the Church of Rome? Not that she requireth works at their hands that will be saved, but that she attributeth unto works a power of satisfying God for sin, and a virtue to merit both grace here and in heaven glory. That this overthroweth the foundation of faith I grant willingly; that it is a direct denial thereof I utterly deny. What it is to hold and what directly to deny the foundation of faith I have already opened. Apply it particularly to this cause, and there needs no more ado. The thing which is handled, if the form under which it is handled be added thereunto, it showeth the foundation of any doctrine whatsoever. Christ is the matter whereof the doctrine of the Gospel treateth, and it treateth of Christ as of a Saviour. Salvation therefore by Christ is the foundation of Christianity. As for works, they are a thing subordinate, no otherwise necessary than because our santification cannot be accomplished without them. The doctrine concerning them is a thing builded upon the foundation; therefore the doctrine which addeth unto them power of satisfying or of meriting addeth unto a thing subordinated, builded upon the foundation, not to the very foundation itself. Yet is the foundation consequently by this addition overthrown, forasmuch as out of this addition it may negatively be concluded, he who maketh any work good and acceptable in the sight of God to proceed from the natural freedom of our will, he who giveth unto any good work of ours the force of satisfying the wrath of God for sin, the power of meriting either earthly or heavenly rewards, he who holdeth works going before our vocation in congruity to merit our vocation, works following our first to merit our second justification and by condignity our last reward in the kingdom of heaven, pulleth up the doctrine of faith by the roots; for out of every of these the plain direct denial thereof may be necessarily concluded. Nor this only, but what other heresy is there which doth not raze the very foundation of faith by consequent?

Differences among heresies

Howbeit, we make a difference of heresies, accounting them in the next degree to infidelity which directly deny any

one thing to be which is expressly acknowledged in the articles of our belief; for out of any one article so denied the
denial of the very foundation itself is straightway inferred.
As, for example, if a man should say, 'There is no Catholic
Church,' it followeth immediately hereupon that this Jesus
whom we call the Saviour is not the Saviour of the world;
because all the prophets bear witness that the true Messias
should 'show a light unto the Gentiles,'[136] that is to say,
gather such a church as is catholic, not restrained any
longer unto one circumcised nation. In a second rank we
place them out of whose positions the denial of any of the
foresaid articles may be with like facility concluded. Such
are they who have denied either the divinity of Christ, with
Ebion, or with Marcion his humanity, an example whereof
may be that of Cassianus defending the incarnation of the
Son of God against Nestorius bishop of Antioch,[137] who held
that the Virgin, when she brought forth Christ, did not bring
forth the Son of God but a sole and mere man;[138] out of which
heresy the denial of the articles of the Christian faith he
deduceth thus:

> If thou dost deny our Lord Jesus Christ to be God, in
> denying the Son thou canst not choose but deny the
> Father; for, according to the voice of the Father
> himself, 'He that hath not the Son hath not the
> Father.'[139] Wherefore denying him that is begotten thou
> deniest him who dost beget. Again, denying the Son of
> God to have been born in the flesh, how canst thou
> believe him to have suffered? Believing not his passion,
> what remaineth but that thou deny his resurrection?
> For we believe him not raised, except we first believe
> him dead; neither can the reason of his rising from the
> dead stand without the faith of his death going before.
> The denial of his death and passion inferreth the denial
> of his rising from the depth. Whereupon it followeth
> that thou also deny his ascension into heaven: the
> Apostle affirming that 'he who ascended did first
> descend.'[140] So that, as much as lieth in thee, our Lord
> Jesus Christ hath neither risen from the depth, nor is
> ascended into heaven, nor sitteth at the right hand of
> God the Father, neither shall he come at the day of final
> account, which is looked for, nor shall judge the quick
> and dead. And darest thou yet set foot in the church?
> Canst thou think thyself a bishop when thou hast

denied all those things whereby thou didst obtain a bishoply calling?[141]

Nestorius confessed all the articles of the creed, but his opinion did imply the denial of every part of his confession.

Heresies there are of a third part, such as the Church of Rome maintaineth, which, being removed by a greater distance from the foundation, although indeed they overthrow it, yet because of that weakness which the philosopher noteth in men's capacities when he saith that the common sort cannot see things which follow in reason, when they follow, as it were, afar off by many deductions; therefore the repugnancy between such heresy and the foundation is not so quickly nor so easily found but that an heretic of this sooner than of the former kind may directly grant, and consequently nevertheless deny, the foundation of faith.

If reason be suspected, trial will show that the Church of Rome doth no otherwise by teaching the doctrine she doth teach concerning works. Offer them the very fundamental words, and what one man is there that will refuse to subscribe unto them? Can they directly grant and deny directly one and the selfsame thing? Our own proceedings in disputing against their works satisfactory and meritorious do show not only that they hold, but that we acknowledge them to hold, the foundation notwithstanding their opinion. For are not these our arguments against them: 'Christ alone hath satisfied and appeased his Father's wrath; Christ hath merited salvation alone'? We should do fondly to use such disputes, neither could we think to prevail by them, if that whereupon we ground were a thing which we know they do not hold, which we are assured they will not grant. Their very answers to all such reasons as are in this controversy brought against them will not permit us to doubt whether they hold the foundation or no. Can any man who hath read their books concerning this matter be ignorant how they draw all their answers unto these heads?

> That the remission of all our sins, the pardon of all whatsoever punishments thereby deserved, the rewards which God hath laid up in heaven, are by the blood of our Lord Jesus Christ purchased and obtained

sufficiently for all men; but for no man effectually for his benefit in particular, except the blood of Christ be applied particularly unto him by such means as God hath appointed it to work by.

That those means of themselves being dead things, only the blood of Christ is that which putteth life, force, and efficacy in them to work, and to be available, each in his kind, to our salvation.

Finally, that grace being purchased for us by the blood of Christ, and freely without any merit or desert at the first bestowed upon us, the good things which we do, after grace received, are made satisfactory and meritorious.

Some of their sentences to this effect I must allege for mine own warrant. If we desire to hear foreign judgments, we find in one this confession:

He that would reckon how many the virtues and merits of our Saviour Jesus Christ have been might likewise understand how many the benefits have been that are come unto us by him, forasmuch as men are made partakers of them all by the mean of his passion: by him is given unto us remission of our sins, grace, glory, liberty, praise, peace, salvation, redemption, justification, justice, sanctification, sacraments, merits, doctrine, and all other things which we had, and were behoveful for our salvation.[142]

In another we have these oppositions and answers made unto them:

All grace is given by Christ Jesus. True; but not except Christ Jesus be applied. He is the propitiation for our sins; by his stripes we are healed; he hath offered up himself for us: all this is true, but apply it.[143] We put all satisfaction in the blood of Jesus Christ; but we hold that the means which Christ hath appointed for us in this case to apply it are our penal works.[144]

Our countrymen in Rheims make the like answer, that they seek salvation no other way than by the blood of Christ, and that humbly they do use prayers, fasting, alms, faith, charity, sacrifice, sacraments, priests, only as the means appointed by Christ, to apply the benefit of his holy blood unto them: touching our good works, that in their own natures they are not meritorious nor answerable unto the joys of heaven; it cometh by the grace of Christ, and not of the work itself, that we have by well-doing a right to heaven and deserve it worthily.

If any men think that I seek to varnish their opinions, to set the better foot of a lame cause foremost, let him know that since I began throughly to understand their meaning I have found their halting in this doctrine greater than perhaps it seemeth to them who know not the deepness of Satan, as the blessed Divine speaketh.[145] For, although this be proof sufficient, that they do not deny directly the foundation of faith, yet, if there were no other leaven in the whole lump of their doctrine but this, this were sufficient to prove that their doctrine is not agreeable with the foundation of Christian faith. The Pelagians, being over-great friends unto nature, made themselves enemies unto grace, for all their confessing that men have their souls and all the faculties thereof, their wills and the ability of their wills, from God. And is not the Church of Rome still an adversary unto Christ's merits, because of her acknowledging that we have received the power of meriting by the blood of Christ? Sir Thomas More setteth down the odds between us and the Church of Rome in the matter of works thus:

> Like as we grant them that no good work of man is rewardable in heaven of his own nature, but through the goodness of God, that list to set so high a price upon so poor a thing, and that this price God setteth through Christ's passion, and for that also they be his own works with us (for good works to God-ward worketh no man, without God work in him); and as we grant them also that no man may be proud of his works for his own imperfect working; and for that in all that man may do he can do no good, but is a servant unprofitable and doth but his bare duty; as we, I say, grant unto them these things, so this one thing or twain do they grant us again, that men are bound to work good works if they have time and power, and that whoso worketh in true faith most shall be most rewarded; but then set they thereto that all his rewards shall be given him for his faith alone, and nothing for his works at all,

because his faith is the thing, they say, and forceth him to work well.[146]

I see by this of Sir Thomas More how easy it is for men of great capacity and judgment to mistake things written or spoken, as well on one side as on another. Their doctrine, as he thought, maketh the works of man rewardable in the world to come through the mere goodness of God, whom it pleaseth to set so high a price upon so poor a thing; and ours, that a man doth receive that eternal and high reward, not for his works, but for his faith's sake by which he worketh; whereas in truth our doctrine is no other than that which we have learned at the feet of Christ: namely, that God doth justify the believing man, yet not for the worthiness of his belief, but for his worthiness who is believed; God rewardeth abundantly everyone who worketh, yet not for any meritorious dignity which is, or can be, in the work, but through his mere mercy, by whose commandment he worketh. Contrariwise, their doctrine is that, as pure water of itself hath no savour, but if it pass through a sweet pipe it taketh a pleasant smell of the pipe through which it passeth, so also, before grace received, our works do neither satisfy nor merit; yet after, they do both the one and the other. Every virtuous action hath then power in such sort to satisfy that if we ourselves commit no mortal sin, no heinous crime, whereupon to spend this treasure of satisfaction in our own behalf, it turneth to the benefit of other men's release on whom it shall please the steward of the house of God to bestow it; so that we may satisfy for ourselves and for others, but merit only for ourselves. In meriting, our actions do work with two hands: with the one they get their morning stipend, the increase of grace; with the other their evening hire, the everlasting crown of glory. Indeed, they teach that our good works do not these things as they come from us, but as they come from grace in us; which grace in us is another thing in their divinity than is the mere goodness of God's mercy toward us in Christ Jesus.[147]

If it were not a strong deluding spirit which hath possesion of their hearts, were it possible but that they should see how plainly they do herein gainsay the very ground of apostolic faith? Is this that salvation by grace whereof so plentiful mention is made in the sacred Scriptures of God? Was this their meaning who first taught the world to look for salvation only by Christ? By grace, the Apostle saith, and by grace in such sort as a gift, a thing that cometh not of ourselves, not of our works, lest any man should boast and say, 'I have wrought out mine own salvation.'[148] By grace they confess; but by grace in such sort that as many as wear the diadem of bliss, they wear nothing but what they have won. The Apostle, as if he had foreseen how the Church of Rome would abuse the world in time by ambiguous terms, to declare in what sense the name of grace must be taken, when we make it the cause of our salvation, saith, 'He saved us according to his mercy';[149] which mercy, although it exclude not the washing of our new birth, the renewing of our hearts by the Holy Ghost, the means, the virtues, the duties which God requireth at their hands who shall be saved, yet it is so repugnant unto merits that to say we are saved for the worthiness of anything which is ours is to deny we are saved by grace. Grace bestoweth freely, and therefore justly requireth the glory of that which is bestowed. We deny the grace of our Lord Jesus Christ, we imbase, disannul, annihilate the benefit of his bitter passion, if we rest in those proud imaginations that life everlasting is deservedly ours, that we merit it, and that we are worthy of it.

Error and heresy not always identical

Howbeit, considering how many virtuous and just men, how many saints, how many martyrs, how many of the ancient fathers of the Church have had their sundry perilous opinions — and among sundry of their opinions this, that they hoped to make God some part of amends for their sins by the voluntary punishments which they laid upon themselves: because by a consequent it may follow hereupon that they were injurious unto Christ, shall we therefore make such deadly epitaphs and set them upon their graves: 'They denied the foundation of faith directly, they are damned, there is no salvation for them'? St. Augustine hath said, *Errare possum, haereticus esse nolo.*[150] And except we put a difference between them that err and them that obstinately persist in error, how is it possible that ever any man should hope to be saved?

Surely, in this case, I have no respect of any person alive or dead. Give me a man, of what estate or condition soever, yea, a cardinal or a pope, whom at the extreme point of his life affliction hath made to know himself, whose heart God hath touched with true sorrow for all his sins, and filled with love toward the Gospel of Christ, whose eyes are opened to see the truth, and his mouth to renounce all heresy and error any way opposite thereunto, this one opinion of merits excepted, which he thinketh God will require at his hands, and because he wanteth, therefore trembleth and is discouraged: 'it may be I am forgetful or unskilful, not furnished with things new and old, as a wise and learned scribe should be,'[151] nor able to allege that whereunto, if it were alleged, he doth bear a mind most willing to yield, and so to be recalled as well from this as from other errors — and shall I think, because of this only error, that such a man toucheth not so much as the hem of Christ's garment? If he do, wherefore should not I have hope that virtue may proceed from Christ to save him? Because his error doth by consequent overthrow his faith shall I therefore cast him off as one who hath utterly cast of Christ, one who holdeth not so much as by a slender thread? No, I will not be afraid to say unto a cardinal or to a pope in this plight, 'Be of good comfort, we have to do with a merciful God, ready to make the best of that little which we hold well, and not with a captious sophister who gathereth the worst out of everything wherein we err.' Is there any reason that I should be suspected, or you offended, for this speech?

Let all affection[152] be laid aside; let the matter be indifferently considered. Is it a dangerous thing to imagine that such men may find mercy? The hour may come when we shall think it a blessed thing to hear that if our sins were as the sins of the pope and cardinals the bowels of the mercy of God are larger. I do not propose unto you a pope with the neck of an emperor under his foot, a cardinal riding his horse to the bridle in the blood of saints, but a pope or a cardinal sorrowful, penitent, disrobed, stripped, not only of usurped power, but also delivered and recalled from error and Antichrist, converted and lying prostrate at the feet of Christ; and shall I think that Christ will spurn him? Shall I cross and gainsay the merciful promises of God generally made unto penitent sinners by opposing the name of a pope or a cardinal? What difference is there between a pope and cardinal, and a John a Style, in this case? If we think it impossible for them, after they be once come within that rank, to be afterwards touched with any such remorse, let that be granted. The Apostle saith, 'If I or an angel from heaven preach unto you,' etc.[153] Let it be as likely that St. Paul or an angel from heaven should preach heresy as that a pope or a cardinal should be brought so far forth to acknowledge the truth; yet if a pope or a cardinal should, what could we find in their persons why they might not be saved?

It is not their persons, you will say, but the error wherein I suppose them to die which excludeth them from hope of mercy: the opinion of merits doth take away all possibility of salvation from them. What, although they hold it only as an error; although they hold the truth soundly and sincerely in all other parts of Christian faith; although they have in some measure all the virtues and graces of the Spirit, all other tokens of God's elect children in them; although they be far from having any proud presumptuous opinion that they shall be saved for the worthiness of their deeds; although the only thing which troubleth and molesteth them be but a little too much dejection, somewhat too great a fear, rising from an erroneous conceit[154] that God will require a worthiness in them which they are grieved to find wanting in themselves; although they be not obstinate in this persuasion; although they be willing and would be glad to forsake it, if any one reason were brought to disprove it; although the only let[155] why they do not forsake it ere they die be the ignorance of the mean whereby it might be disproved; although the cause why the ignorance in this point is not removed be the want of knowledge in such as should be able, and are not, to remove it? Let me die if ever it be proved that simply an error doth exclude a pope or a cardinal, in such a case, utterly from hope of life. Surely, I must confess unto you, if it be an error to think that God may be merciful to save men even when they err, my greatest comfort is my error: were it not for the love I bear unto this error, I would neither wish to speak nor to live.

Wherefore, to resume that mother-sentence, whereof I little thought that so much trouble would have grown, 'I doubt not but God was merciful to save thousands of our fathers living in popish superstitions, inasmuch as they sinned ignorantly': alas, what bloody matter is there contained in this sentence that it should be an occasion of so many hard censures! Did I say that 'thousands of our fathers might be saved'? I have showed which way it cannot be denied. Did I say, 'I doubt it not but they were saved'? I see no impiety in this persuasion, though I had no reason in the world for it. Did I say, 'Their ignorance doth make me hope they did find mercy and so were saved'? What doth hinder salvation but sin? Sins are not equal; and ignorance, though it do not make sin to be no sin, yet, seeing it did make their sin the less, why should it not make our hope concerning their life the greater? We pity the most, and I doubt not but God hath most compassion over, them that sin for want of under-standing. As much is confessed by sundry others, almost in the selfsame words which I have used. It is but only my ill hap that the same sentences which favour verity in other men's books should seem to bolster heresy when they are once by me recited.[156] If I be deceived in this point, not they but the blessed Apostle hath deceived me. What I said of others, the same he saith of himself: 'I obtained mercy, for I did it ignorantly.'[157] Construe his words, and ye cannot misconstrue mine. I speak no otherwise, I meant no otherwise.

Thus have I brought the question concerning our fathers at the length unto an end; of whose estate, upon so fit an oc-casion as was offered me, handling the weighty causes of separation between the Church of Rome and us, and the weak motives which commonly are brought to retain men in that society, amongst which motives the example of our fathers deceased is one; although I saw it convenient to ut-ter that sentence which I did, to the end that all men might thereby understand how untruly we are said to condemn as many as have been before us otherwise persuaded than we ourselves are; yet more than one sentence I did not think it expedient to utter, judging it a great deal meeter for us to have regard to our own estate than to sift over curiously what is become of other men; and fearing lest that such questions as this, if voluntarily they should be too far wad-ed in, might seem worthy of that rebuke which our Saviour thought needful in a case not unlike: 'What is this unto thee?'[158] When as I was forced, much besides mine expecta-tion, to render a reason of my speech, I could not but yield at the call of others to proceed as duty bound me for the fuller satisfaction of men's minds. Wherein I have walked, as with reverence, so with fear: with reverence in regard of our fathers who lived in former times; not without fear, considering them that are alive.

I am not ignorant how ready men are to feed and soothe up themselves in evil. Shall I (will the man say that loveth the present world more than he loveth Christ), shall I incur the high displeasure of the mightiest upon earth, shall I hazard my goods, endanger my estate, put my life in jeopardy, rather than yield to that which so many of my fathers have embraced, and yet found favour in the sight of God? 'Curse Meroz, saith the Lord, curse her inhabitants because they help not the Lord, they help him not against the mighty.'[159] If I should not only not help the Lord against the mighty, but help to strengthen them that are mighty against the Lord, worthily might I fall under the burden of that curse, worthy I were to bear my own judgment. But if the doctrine which I teach be a flower gathered in the garden of the Lord, a part of the saving truth of the Gospel, from whence notwithstanding poisoned creatures do suck venom, I can but wish it were otherwise and content myself with the lot that hath befallen me, the rather because it hath not befallen me alone. St. Paul did preach a truth, and a comfortable truth, when he taught that the greater our misery is in respect of our iniquities the readier is the mercy of our God for our release, if we seek unto him; the more we have sinned, the more praise and glory and honour unto him that pardoneth our sin.

But mark what lewd collections were made hereupon by some: 'Why then am I condemned for a sinner?' And, saith the Apostle, 'as we are blamed and as some affirm that we say, why do we not evil that good may come of it?'[160] He was accused to teach that which ill-disposed men did gather by his teaching, though it were clean not only beside but also against his meaning. The Apostle addeth: 'Their condemnation who thus do is just.' I am not hasty to apply sentences of condemnation: I wish from my heart their conversion, whosoever are thus perversely affected. For I must needs say, their case is fearful, their estate dangerous, who harden themselves, presuming on the mercy of God towards others. It is true that God is merciful, but let us

beware of presumptuous sins.[161] God delivered Jonah from
the bottom of the sea: will you therefore cast yourselves
headlong from the tops of rocks and say in your hearts, 'God
shall deliver us'?[162] He pitieth the blind that would gladly
see; but will God pity him that may see and hardeneth
himself in blindness? No; Christ hath spoken too much unto
you for you to claim the privilege of your fathers.

As for us that have handled this cause concerning the
condition of our fathers, whether it be this thing or any
other which we bring unto you, the counsel is good which
the wise man giveth: 'Stand thou fast in thy sure understanding, in the way and knowledge of the Lord, and have
but one manner of word, and follow the word of peace and
righteousness.'[163] As a loose tooth is a great grief unto him
that eateth, so doth a wavering and unstable word, in
speech that tendeth to instruction, offend. 'Shall a wise
man speak words of the wind,' saith Eliphaz—light, incon-
stant, unstable words?[164] Surely the wisest may speak words
of the wind: such is the untoward constitution of our nature
that we neither do so perfectly understand the way and
knowledge of the Lord, nor so steadfastly embrace it when
it is understood, nor so graciously utter it when it is embraced, nor so peaceably maintain it when it is uttered, but
that the best of us are overtaken sometimes through blindness, sometimes through hastiness, sometimes through
impatience, sometimes through other passions of the
mind, whereunto (God doth know) we are too subject.

We must therefore be contented both to pardon others
and to crave that others may pardon us for such things. Let
no man who speaketh as a man think himself (whilst he
liveth) always freed from scapes and oversights in his
speech. The things themselves which I have spoken unto
you I hope are sound, howsoever they have seemed otherwise unto some, at whose hands if I have, in that respect,
received injury, I willingly forget it; although, in truth, considering the benefit which I have reaped by this necessary
search of truth, I rather incline unto that of the Apostle,
'They have not injured me at all.'[165] I have cause to wish, and
I do wish them as many blessings in the kingdom of heaven
as they have forced me to utter words and syllables in this
cause, wherein I could not be more sparing in speech than
I have been. 'It becometh no man,' saith St. Jerome, 'to be

patient in the crime of heresy.'[166] Patient, as I take it, we should be always, though the crime of heresy were intended; but silent in a thing of so great consequence I could not, beloved, I durst not be; especially the love which I bear to the truth in Christ Jesus being hereby somewhat called in question. Whereof I beseech them, in the meekness of Christ,[167] that have been the first original cause, to consider that a watchman may cry 'An enemy!' when indeed a friend cometh. In which case, as I deem such a watchman to be more worthy to be loved for his care than misliked for his error, so I have judged it my own part in this case, as much as in me lieth, to take away all suspicion of any unfriendly intent or meaning against the truth, from which, God doth know, my heart is free.

Now to you, beloved, who have heard these things I will use no other words of admonition than those which are offered me by St. James: 'My brethren, have not this faith of our glorious Lord Jesus Christ in respect of persons.'[168] Ye are not now to learn that, as of itself it is not hurtful, so neither should it be to any man scandalous and offensive, in doubtful cases, to hear the different judgment of men. Be it that Cephas hath one interpretation and Apollos hath another, that Paul is of this mind and Barnabas of that; if this offend you, the fault is yours. Carry peaceable minds, and ye may have comfort by this variety.

Now the God of peace give you peaceable minds and turn it to your everlasting comfort!

Footnotes

[1]G. Lechler, *John Wycliffe and His English Precursors*, trans. Peter Lorimer, (London: C. Kegan Paul & Co., 1878), p. 234.

[2]This emphasis on Scripture is found in many places in his writings, but see especially his work *De veritate scripturae sacrae (On the Truth of Holy Scripture)*.

[3]*De dominio divino (On Divine Lordship)*, I, iii, 2.

[4]*Ibid.*, III, iv, 4.

[5]By "This Man," of course, he means Christ, *ibid.*, III, iv, 5.

[6]Sermons, see Lechler, *op. cit.*, p. 287, n. 1.

[7]John Foxe records a number of these prosecutions in some detail in Book V of his *Acts and Monuments*, (1843; reprint ed., New York: AMS Press 1965).

[8]A. G. Dickens, *Lollards and Protestants in the Diocese of York, 1509-1558*, (Oxford: Oxford University Press, 1959), pp. 7f.

[9]W. A. Clebsch, *England's Earliest Protestants 1520-1535*, (New Haven, CT: Yale University Press, n.d.), p. 4.

[10]John Foxe, *Acts and Monuments*, Book V; see the 1843, London, edition, Vol. III, pp. 257f. I have modernized the spelling and some of the terminology. The text given by Foxe is that "copied out and corrected," i.e. modernized by William Tyndale in his day; see *Ibid.*, p. 249.

[11]E. Harris Harbison, *The Christian Scholar in the Age of the Reformation*, (New York: Scribner, 1956), p. 58.

[12]F. Seebohm, *The Oxford Reformers*, (London: Longmans, Green & Co., 1914), p. 16.

[13]John Colet, *Lectures on Romans*, trans. J.H. Lupton, (1873; reprint ed., Ridgewood, N.J.: The Gregg Press, 1965), p. 8.

[14]*Ibid.*, pp. 8f.

[15]*Ibid.*, p. 20.

[16]*Ibid.*, p. 40.

[17]*Ibid.*, p. 49.

[18]*Christ's Mystical Body, the Church*, in *Letters to Radulphus, etc.*, trans. J.H. Lupton, (1876; reprint ed., Ridgewood, N.J.: The Gregg Press, 1965), p. 32.

[19]*Lectures on Romans*, p. 29; cf. 1 Jn. 4:7.

[20]*Exposition of Romans*, a commentary on the first five chapters of the epistle only, and a later work than the Oxford lectures, in *Letters to Radulphus, etc.*, as above, p. 126.

[21]*Lectures on Romans*, p. 16.

[22]*Christ's Mystical Body*, pp. 32f.

[23]See J.H. Lupton, *A Life of John Colet, D.D.*, 3rd ed., (Hamden, CT.: Shoe,

String Press, 1961), p. 114; F. Seebohm, *The Oxford Reformers*, 3rd ed., (Longmans, Green & Co., 1887), pp. 137f.

[24]John Foxe, *Acts and Monuments*, Vol. V, pp. 114f.

[25]J.H. Lupton, *op. cit.*, pp. 185, 187.

[26]W. A. Clebsch, *op. cit.*, p. 46.

[27]*The Colloquies of Erasmus*, trans. Craig R. Thomson, (Chicago: University of Chicago Press, 1965), p. 305, where Colet is pseudonymously spoken of as "an Englishmen named Gratian Pullus, a learned and upright man."

[28]John Foxe, *op cit.*, IV, p. 230.

[29]Hugh Latimer, *Sermons*, Parker Society ed., (Cambridge: Cambridge University Press, 1844), p. 440.

[30]Ps. 51:8.

[31]Rom. 3:22-24. John Foxe, *op. cit.*, IV, pp. 635f.

[32]John Foxe, *ibid.*, p. 620.

[33]John Foxe, *ibid.*, p. 651.

[34]John Foxe, *ibid.*, p. 620.

[35]The work was a response to what John Ashwell, the prior of Newnham Abbey in Bedfordshire, had written to the Bishop of Lincoln accusing Joye of Lutheran sympathies. See W. A. Clebsch, *op. cit.*, pp. 214ff.; D. B. Knox, *The Doctrine of Faith in the Reign of Henry VIII*, (London: James Clarke & Co., 1961), pp. 55 ff.

[36]Cited by D. B. Knox, *op. cit.*, p. 56.

[37]Cited by W. A. Clebsch, *op. cit.*, p. 215. I have modernized the spelling.

[38]Acts 4:12; 13:39; 1 Jn. 2:2; 4:10.

[39]Rev. 5:1-10.

[40]Rom. 11:6.

[41]Eph. 2:8f.

[42]Robert Barnes, *Treatise on Justification, or Only Faith Justifieth before God*. The edition I have used is that issued by the Religious Tract Society in London (undated, but in the nineteenth century) of the Writings of John Frith and Robert Barnes, pp. 99ff.

[43]The translation is that given in *Creeds of the Churches*, ed. John H. Leith, (Garden City, N.Y.: Doubleday & Co., 1963), pp. 69ff.

[44]William Tyndale, *Doctrinal Treatises*, Parker Society ed., (Cambridge: Cambridge University Press, 1848), p. 46.

[45]Ibid., pp. 50f.

[46]*Ibid.*, p. 53.

[47]*Ibid.*, p. 56. This notion is echoed in Barnes' *Treatise on Justification;* see pp. 16f. above.

[48]1 Jn. 3:9.

[49]William Tyndale, *op. cit.*, p. 126.

[50]*Ibid.*, p. 90.

[51]*Ibid.*, pp. 63-66.

[52]*Ibid.*, p. 77.

[53]*Ibid.*, p. 90.

[54]*Op. cit.*, pp. 508f.

[55]Gilbert Burnet, *The History of the Reformation of the Church of England*, first published 1679-1714; new ed., (Oxford: Oxford University Press, 1865), Vol. I, p. 406; Vol. III, p. 212.

[56]G. Burnet, *op. cit.*, Vol. I, pp. 344f.

[57]The reference is not to those of the early church but to the desire to hold a modern council.

[58]G. Burnet, *op. cit.*, Vol. I, pp. 424f., 283, 288.

[59]John Strype, *Memorials of Archbishop Cranmer*, 1694; Ecclesiastical History Society ed., (Oxford: Oxford University Press, 1848), Vol. II, p. 17.

[60]J. T. Tomlinson, *The Prayer Book, Articles, and Homilies*, (London: Elliot Stock, 1897), pp. 230ff.

[61]The ninth homily, "An Exhortation against the Fear of Death," is also probably a composition of Cranmer's. See J. T. Tomlinson, *op. cit.*, pp. 232f.

[62]These "postils" were homiletical expositions of the Epistles and Gospels appointed for the Sundays and major festivals of the Christian year.

[63]See D. B. Knox, *op. cit.*, pp. 212f.

[64]Acts 4:12.

[65]*Certain Sermons or Homilies appointed to be read in Churches*, 1899 edn., containing both books of Homilies, pp. 438–442.

[66]Cf. Is. 53:5, 8, 12.

[67]*Loc. cit.*, pp. 451, 453.

[68]*Ibid.*, pp. 457f.

[69]*Ibid.*, p. 464.

[70]*Ibid.*, p. 440.

[71]*Ibid.*, pp. 466ff.; cf. Rom. 6.

[72]*Certain Homilies*, as above, pp. 20f.

[73]Rom 3:23; 10:4; and 8:3f.

[74]As is declared in Eph. 2:8, which Cranmer quotes.

[75]*Op. cit.*, pp. 22f.

[76]*Ibid.*, pp. 24–26.

[77]*Ibid.*, pp. 22f.

[78]*Ibid.*, p. 25.

[79]*Ibid.*, pp. 30f. See Tit. 1:16; Jas. 2:17ff.

[80]*Ibid.*, p. 27.

[81]Concerning the influence of the Württemberg Confession of 1552 on the doctrinal formulations in some of the articles, including Article 11 in its later form, see E. Tyrrell Green, *The Thirty-nine Articles and the Age of the Reformation: an Historical and Doctrinal Exposition in the Light of Contemporary Documents*, London, 1896, Index p. 456, *sub. voc.*, and the references given there; William A. Curtis, *A History of Creeds and Confessions of Faith*, Edinburgh, 1911, pp. 180f.; also *The Harmony of Protestant Confessions*, London, 1844, pp. 203ff., where the text of chapter 5 and 7 of the Württemberg Confession on Justification and Good Works respectively are given; this volume is a new edition, revised and enlarged by Peter Hall, of the *Harmonia Confessionum Orthodoxarum et Reformatarum Ecclesiarum*, first published in Geneva in 1581, the English translation of which was first brought out in 1586 at Cambridge.

[82]Cf. Heb. 4:13.

[83]Augustine, *De Gratia et Libero Arbitrio*, 17: "God begins his influence by working in us that we may have the will, and completes it by working with us when we have the will . . . We can, however, ourselves do nothing to effect good works of piety without him either working that we may will, or working with us when we have the will."

[84]Eph. 2:1–10; Phil. 2:13.

[85]2 Cor. 3:18.

[86]1 Jn. 3:2f.

[87]Heb. 4:15; 7:26; 2 Cor. 5:21; 1 Pet. 2:22; 1 Jn. 3:5.

[88]1 Jn. 1:8.

[89]Article 12.

[90]Lk. 17:10.

[91]John Strype, *Memorials of Archbishop Cranmer*, as above, Vol. III, p. 111.

[92]J. E. Booty, ed., *An Apology of the Church of England by John Jewel*, (Ithaca, N.Y.: Cornell University Press, 1963), pp. xliv, xlv.

93*The Works of John Jewel,* Parker Society ed., (Cambridge: Cambridge University Press, 1848), Vol. III, p. 56.
94 2 Tim. 3:16f.
95*Loc. cit.,* p. 57.
96See 1 Tim. 2:5; Jn 14:6, 13; 15:16; 16:23.
97John Jewel, *Loc. cit.,* pp. 65f.
98*Ibid.,* p. 66; Rom. 13:13; Phil. 2:12; Col. 1:13; Heb. 9:14; Eph. 2:10; 1 Cor. 6:19f.; Eph. 3:17.
99Rom. 3:24, 28; Gal. 2:16.
100*Loc. cit.,* pp. 243f. Gregory of Nazianzus' Greek expression *to pisteusai monon* is taken as the equivalent of *sola fides.* It may well be, however, that Jewel was here citing passages already sought out by Cranmer, see p. 53 below.
101Richard Hooker, *Works,* arranged by John Keble, Vol. III, (Oxford: Clarendon Press, 1888), pp. 689f.; Ps. 115:1; 1 Cor. 1:31.
102Gen. 15:6; Rom. 4:3.
103Ps. 32:1.
104Rom. 8:33.
105R. Hooker, *loc. cit.,* pp. 693f.
106Pp. 61ff.
107Izaac Walton, *The Life of Mr. Richard Hooker,* in Keble's edition of Hooker's works. Vol. I, p. 51.

Footnotes for Part II

1Rom. 3:20,24; Gal. 2:16
2Cf. Ps. 85:10.
3Rom. 3:23-25.
4Rom. 10:4.
5Rom. 8:3f.
6Eph. 2:8f. It should be noticed that "justice" is often used in the sense of "righteousness" by Cranmer and Hooker and their contemporaries.
7Cf. Eph. 2:10.
8Gal. 3:21.
9Gal. 2:21.
10Gal. 5:4.
11Eph. 2:8f.
12Acts 10:43.
13Phil. 3:9.
14Gal. 2:16.
15Jn. 1:29.
16Gal. 2:16.
17Gal. 5:6; 1 Thess. 1:3; 2 Thess. 1:11; 1 Tim. 6:12; Jas. 2:17.
18Jas. 2:19.

Footnotes for Part III

1 1 Cor. 5:12f.
2 1 Cor. 5:13.
3 2 Cor. 6:14.
4The quotation that follows has not been traced, but it probably comes from a treatise or homily wrongly attributed to Eusebius of Emesa.
5 1 Tim. 2:6.

[6] 2 Cor. 5:14f.; Eph. 2:1, 5.
[7] That is, righteousness.
[8] 1 Cor. 1:30.
[9] Rom. 8:21.
[10] See Council of Trent, sess. V., decree concerning original sin, 4.
[11] See Council of Trent, sess. VI., ch. 7.
[12] *Ibid.*
[13] See Council of Trent, sess. VI., ch. 4, 5; canons 4, 9.
[14] See Council of Trent, sess. VI., ch. 10.
[15] See Council of Trent, sess. VI., chs. 14, 15.
[16] See Council of Trent, sess. VI., ch. 14.
[17] Phil. 3:8f.
[18] 2 Cor. 5:21.
[19] Rom. 4:5.
[20] 1 Jn. 3:7.
[21] Rom. 4.
[22] Jas. 2:18ff.
[23] Rom. 6:22.
[24] Hab. 1:4.
[25] Cf. Mt. 5:21f.
[26] That is, with any secondary or ulterior motive.
[27] Gen. 18:23ff.
[28] Ps. 119:5.
[29] Rom. 7:19, 24.
[30] Is. 1:4.
[31] Heb. 1:1–4; Ps. 79; 106:41ff.
[32] That is, inference.
[33] Acts 13:42.
[34] For centuries Paul had been accepted as the author of this epistle, and Hooker does not question this view here, though in the early centuries the matter had been much disputed and earlier in the sixteenth century the Pauline authorship had been rejected by scholars such as Erasmus, Luther and Calvin.
[35] Heb. 1:2.
[36] Cf. 1 Cor. 3:11ff.
[37] Rev. 18:4.
[38] Mt. 24:15ff.; Mk. 13:14ff.; Lk. 21:21ff.
[39] Gen. 19:15.
[40] That is, usage.
[41] *i.e.,* preachers and teachers.
[42] Jude 22.
[43] Heb. 6:9.
[44] Jn. 3:17f.
[45] Rev. 2:21–23.
[46] See 1 Cor. 3:10–15.
[47] Jerome, *Adversus Helvidium*, 21.
[48] 1 Tim. 3:16.
[49] Jn. 1:49.
[50] Jn. 4:42.
[51] See Rev. 2:9; 3:9.
[52] See Ez. 23.
[53] Gal. 5:2.
[54] The reference is no doubt to the Lutheran doctrine of consubstantiation.
[55] Rev. 3:8.
[56] Lk. 13:3.
[57] Ps. 19:12.

[58]Gal. 5:2, 4.
[59]2 Thess. 2:10-12.
[60]Sc. the beast wielding the authority of Antichrist.
[61]Rev. 13:8.
[62]Rom. 10:10.
[63]That is, righteousness.
[64]Rom. 8:15f.
[65]See Gal. 5:22; 1 Cor. 12:6, 11, KJV.
[66]1 Cor. 3:16f.; 6:19.
[67]See Gen. 5:24; Heb. 11:5; Job 1:8; Lk. 1:5f.
[68]Sc. belief, faith, adoption.
[69]Confession of Württemberg, ch. 7.
[70]Eph. 1:22f.; 2:20-22; 4:15f.; 1 Pet. 2:4ff.
[71]Eph. 2:20.
[72]Jn. 6:69.
[73]Tim. 3:15.
[74]Cf. Lk. 10:25; Acts 16:30.
[75]Mt. 11:12.
[76]Acts 16:17.
[77]Heb. 10:20.
[78]Heb. 11:4-22.
[79]Job 19:23-27.
[80]Lk. 1:70; 24:25f., 44-47.
[81]Cf. Lk. 1:28-32.
[82]Gen. 22:18; Gal. 3:16.
[83]Acts 4:12.
[84]Lk. 1:34f.; 2:25ff.
[85]1 Cor. 3:11.
[86]Acts 25:18f.
[87]That is, refute.
[88]See Jas. 2:19.
[89]Minucius Felix, Octavius, 34.
[90]Rom. 8:10, KJV.
[91]Phil. 2:16; 1 Jn. 1:1.
[92]Col. 3:4.
[93]1 Pet. 1:23
[94]Eph. 2:1-6.
[95]1 Jn. 5:12.
[96]Rom. 6:9.
[97]Rom. 6:11
[98]Mt. 28:20.
[99]1 Pet. 1:23.
[100]1 Jn. 3:9.
[101]Eph. 1:14; 2 Cor. 1:22.
[102]Jn. 14:16f.
[103]1 Thess. 5:19.
[104]Lk. 12:32.
[105]Col. 1:23
[106]1 Tim. 2:15.
[107]Jn. 10:28.
[108]1 Cor. 10:6ff.; Heb. 3:7ff.
[109]Rev. 2:4.
[110]1 Jn. 3:9.
[111]Dt. 32:10; Ps. 17:80
[112]Mt. 26:69ff.
[113]For reference and comment v. Keble, p. 519.

[114]Lk. 22:31f.

[115]Dt. 6:13; Mt. 4:10.

[116]Gal. 4:15.

[117]Gal. 1:6.

[118]Phil. 3:2.

[119]Acts 15:5.

[120]Gal. 4:9, 21ff., 31.

[121]Gal. 4:10f.

[122]Gal. 5:2,4.

[123]Quotation apparently attributed to Bucer, *De unitate ecclesiae servanda*, by Hooker; but unidentified by Keble, p. 523.

[124]J. Calvin, Letter to Laelius Socinus, 9 Dec. 1549, (Brunswick; C.A. Schwetschke, 1875), Epistola 1324, *Opera quae supersunt omnia*, vol. XIII, col. 487; cf. *Inst.* IV, ii, 11f.

[125]Rev. 13:16; 14:9.

[126]That is, Calvin.

[127]Phillipe de Morney du Plessis, *Tractatus de ecclesia*, Geneva, 1585, ch. 2, pp. 32f.

[128]Zanchius, *De religione christiana*, in the prefatory epistle dedicating the work to Ulysses Martinengo.

[129]A tenant paravail was the lowest tenant or subtenant, at the other end of the scale from the lord paramount (as the vale or valley is from the mount).

[130]Cf. Gal. 2:9.

[131]Cf. Thess. 2:13.

[132]Mt. 5:20.

[133]Cf. Mt. 23:23-26.

[134]Cf. Mt. 5:21ff.

[135]Cf. Eph. 1:3ff.

[136]Cf. Lk. 2:32; Act 26:23.

[137]Actually bishop of Constantinople.

[138]Nestorius, as we now know, did not teach this heresy with which his name for so long has been connected.

[139]See I Jn. 2:23.

[140]Eph. 4:9.

[141]John Cassian, *De incarnatione Domini contra Nestorium*, VI, 17f.

[142]Lewis of Granada; for reference and annotations see p. 536 in Keble's edition (Vol. III).

[143]Cf. 1 Jn. 2:2; Is. 53:5; 1 Pet. 2:24; Heb. 7:27; 9:14; 10:12.

[144]Francis Panigarola; reference and annotations as in note 142.

[145]Rev. 2:24.

[146]Thomas More, *A Dialogue of Comfort*, I, 12; *The Complete Works of St. Thomas More*, ed. L. L. Martz and F. Manley, Vol. 12, (New Haven, CT: Yale University Press, 1976), p. 39.

[147]Keble, pp. 538f., cites a passage from Panigarola which Hooker apparently had in mind; see also the Council of Trent, Session VI, chs. 7 and 10.

[148]Eph. 2:8f.; the injunction of Phil. 2:12, 'work out your own salvation,' is not a contradiction of Eph. 2:8f., not an exhortation to save oneself by one's works, but a challenge to put one's salvation to work, with the assurance which is immediately added, 'for God is at work in you, both to will and to work for his good pleasure'—God, that is to say, is the source not only of the believer's good work but even of his good will which motivates his good work.

[149]Tit. 3:5.

[150]'I can be in error, but I have no wish to be a heretic.' The quotation had previously appeared in Jewel's *Defence* of his *Apology of the Church of England*, (Vol. III, p. 210), though with *non possum* instead of *nolo*, and it

reappears in Pilkington (Parker Society edn., p. 610) and Whitgift (I, p. 8; II, p. 539; III, p. 460), both of whom, together with Hooker, probably derived it from Jewel, a veritable fountain of patristic learning. Though the precise quotation has not been located in Augustine's works, teaching to this effect occurs in a number of places in his writings.

[151]Mt. 13:52.
[152]That is, sentiment or predispostion.
[153] Gal. 1:8.
[154]That is, conception.
[155]That is, hindrance.
[156]Cf. the opinion of Calvin, etc., cited above, pp. 92ff.
[157]1 Tim. 1:13.
[158]Jn. 21:22.
[159]Judg. 5:23.
[160]Rom. 3:7f.
[161]Ps. 19:13.
[162]Cf. Mt. 4:5-7.
[163]Ecclus. 5:10.
[164]Job 15:2.
[165]2 Cor. 2:5, 10.
[166]Jerome, *Against John of Jerusalem*, 2 J. P. Migne, *Patrologioe Latinae*, Vol. XXIIII,; more literally, 'when under suspicion of heresy.'
[167]Cf. 2 Cor. 10:1.
[168]Jas. 2:1.